MY SCOTTISH COMI

MY SCOTTISH COMMON PEOPLE

GEORGE SMITH

YOUCAXTON PUBLICATIONS

OXFORD & SHREWSBURY

ISBN 978-1-912419-23-4
Printed and bound in Great Britain.
Published by YouCaxton Publications 2018

YouCaxton Publications
enquiries@youcaxton.co.uk

In loving memory of
George and Doris

Preface

My Scottish Common People is an account of the lives of my forebears. All of them   lived in Scotland, the country of their birth. They were largely people without the benefit of property ownership or wealth. They possessed little or no power. They were ordinary people. The title of this book was suggested by Alison Light's *Common People*, for my family history has echoes of her family history. It differs by having a Scottish context rather than English one. However, I see much similarity between the two accounts.

My initial interest in my forebears was probably sparked off by the distance between me and the country they inhabited. My family moved from Dundee to Manchester in 1949, when I was aged four, and then we moved from Manchester to London in 1958. Subsequently, I have lived in several places in England. Living in England from childhood, it was not easy to wise up on my predecessors. From my parents, I acquired a smattering of knowledge about a few forebears who were in their memory. From relatives who were visited during holidays in Dundee, that knowledge was enlarged. But there was a dearth of artefacts handed down by my forebears. Moreover, because my paternal grand-parents had died before I was aged two, an important source of family knowledge was closed to me. All told, my family history resembled a big black hole lit by a handful of flickering stars. These circumstances promoted my curiosity about the people who had gone before me. Just who were they? My first attempt as an adult to answer that question occurred in 1973. I was on holiday in Orkney and decided spontaneously to learn something of my Orcadian forebears. From Orkney mainland, I travelled to the island of Westray, where I obtained permission to inspect the statutory registers in the school where they were kept. I searched the registers and made notes on possible ancestors. However, afterwards, I made no follow up. I was not sure of the next steps and my interest fizzled out for a while.

My parents died in 1978 and 1982 and after their deaths, my curiosity about my forebears increased. In those pre-internet days, I recognised that the obvious way to satisfy my curiosity was to make a search of the genealogical records that were archived in Edinburgh. I could see that there were a number of barriers that I had to overcome to do that. The most formidable of these was acquiring the know-how to do genealogical research. Instead of a visit to Edinburgh, I hit upon an alternative way that was more feasible in several respects. I asked the Scots Ancestry Research Society, for a fee, to investigate for me. Between 1987 and 1995, the Society produced separate reports on the paternal lines of my four grandparents. The reports were informative in their genealogical details and that gave me some satisfaction. I acquired a sense of my roots. However, with the passage of time, my curiosity increased further. Various questions emerged in my mind about my forebears from the bare facts that had been produced. I wanted to put much more historical flesh on the genealogical bones. But I did not feel that I could do that because family and work commitments made it difficult to realise.

It was only when I reached retirement and the freedom that it offered that I decided to satisfy a lingering curiosity by personally researching my family history. I considered that my existing research skills equipped me fairly well for my proposed project. I was a former academic in social studies with a PhD. But I still felt a need to tailor my research skills more specifically to family history. To fulfil my aspiration, in 2013, I began the post-graduate certificate in family and local history by distance learning at Dundee University. I was energised by starting the certificate course and after completing three modules satisfactorily, I felt capable of carrying out a plan of research without completing the whole course.

My plan was to extend, where possible, the four paternal lines that had been started by the Scots Ancestry Research Society, to research the four corresponding maternal lines as far back as possible and to uncover the family history of all eight lines. I also started the research with several questions in mind. I wanted to know about my paternal grandfather's life as a trade unionist and socialist in the early 1900s. What was my maternal grandfather's experience in the Royal Artillery in WW1? Was my Stornoway-born great grandmother of Hebridean ancestry? What was life like for my Orcadian forebears and what had prompted their migration to Dundee? I wanted to solve the mystery of a Dundonian forebear's sojourn in India in the late 1800s. Could I get a more detailed description of the lives of my two namesakes, who toiled on the land in rural Angus in the early 1800s? I hoped to learn about a forbear's passage in the Breadalbane Fencibles during the French revolutionary war.

As my research progressed, I found answers to my initial questions and discovered more forebears. The acquisition of more information also suggested new lines of thought about my ancestors. When I came to research my parents, last of all, I sought to fill in gaps in my knowledge of their lives before I was born and during my early childhood. Because my father was a trade union leader with a public profile, I sought to explore sources that would inform me about the public man to complement my personal knowledge of him. I wondered if trade union records and historical sources would tell me a different story about him to the one I already knew.

In my research, I have consulted a wide range of sources both printed and virtual. I have visited six archives and several libraries. I have provided a bibliography to authenticate my research but I have not provided an annotated list of references because I have written this book for the general reader rather than the scholar.

Although I have uncovered much of my family history, I have not completed it for I still have questions that I would like answered and I expect to continue with my investigation. I believe that family history is always a work in progress.

I have attempted to offer an account of my forebears that is even handed to the men and women. However, there may appear to be some gender lop-sidedness because of greater brevity in the description of the lives of female forebears. That has arisen because the lives of working class women were more private than public and this is reflected in records and historical accounts.

My Scottish Common People starts with two chapters on my most recent forebears, my parents. The eight direct ancestral lines that they brought together are then described separately in the chapters that follow. I have identified each ancestral line by a prominent characteristic of that line. These characteristics have been used as the titles of chapters.

Chapter 1 describes the lives of my parents in Dundee and Manchester, my father's progression from shipyard joiner and lay union official to full-time union officer and accompanying changes in his political affiliation.

In chapter 2, my parents' time in London is described. It includes my father as a union general secretary and member of the TUC's inner circle, his alcoholism and recovery, his promotion of union reform and support for the Labour party.

In chapter 3, an outline is given of my experience in tracking eight family lines that George and Doris brought together.

Chapter 4 tells the story of the paternal forebears of my paternal grandfather. Events in their lives in rural Angus included intermittent reliance on poor relief, conscription into the militia, gaining possession of a plot of land and leaving the land for the town.

Chapter 5 describes the grassroots political and trade union activities of my paternal grandfather. A shoe clicker, exempted from conscription, he opposed WW1 and experienced spells of unemployment in his native Arbroath and in Dundee.

Chapter 6 addresses the maternal line of my paternal grandfather. This line originated in Inverness-shire in the Highlands. These

Gaelic-speaking forebears, like many of their peers, left the Highlands for farm work in the Lowlands.

Chapter 7 describes the paternal line of my paternal grandmother. These ardent Presbyterians from Perthshire disputed the established religious order from the early 1700s and subsequently extended their dispute to the established political order.

In chapter 8, the maternal line of my paternal grandmother is described. These females, who originated from Fife, sewed to make and mend clothes at home in the 1700s and in the 1800s their domestic activity became paid work.

In chapter 9, a description is given of the maternal line of my maternal grandmother. These forebears, for hundreds of years, inhabited the sea-faring village of Broughty Ferry on the river Tay, where salmon catching was a traditional activity.

Chapter 10 is about the paternal line of my maternal grandmother. These forebears from rural Angus came to Dundee in its early days as a textile town. They experienced its growth as a seaport and its jute making heyday.

In chapter 11, an account is given of my maternal grandfather's paternal line. These forebears farmed and fished on the island of Westray in Orkney from the time of the Norse settlement.

In chapter 12, my maternal grandfather's maternal line is described. These peasant forebears lived for centuries on the sheep-ridden, seaweed collecting, sandy- beached island of Sanday in Orkney.

The investigation of my family history started a long time ago and has gained in pace in the last few years. I have learned much about the lives (and times) of my forebears, of whom I knew so little at the start. Because I have made many unexpected discoveries and uncovered lives that contrast so much with my own, the experience has been truly fascinating. It is for that reason that I have written *My Scottish Common People*. I hope that you will share my fascination.

Acknowledgements

I thank Eva Catlow and Eric Smith for their memories of our forebears, their encouragement and interest. I thank Una Harper and the late Stewart Smith for their memories of my paternal grandfather. I thank Betty Mills for sharing documentation and her knowledge of our Ferguson forebears.

In searching the records and other sources at Angus Archives, Perth and Kinross Archives, National Records of Scotland and the National Archives, I was much assisted by staff. At Dundee City Archives, Iain Flett was very helpful, particularly regarding Dundee's history as a port.

The Royal Artillery Museum helped me by identifying the war diary for my maternal grandfather's military service.

I was helped by staff at the Modern Records Centre, University of Warwick, who gave me access to its trade union records.

The Libraries of Birmingham University and Warwick University facilitated my access to publications on politics and the history of industrial relations. Dundee Central Library made available to me publications on local history.

Olwyn and Barrie Jack of the Tay Valley Family History Society helped to elucidate the genealogy and family history of the people of Broughty Ferry.

John Cartmell was helpful by his comments on a draft of the book.

Contents

A Note on Trade Unions

In this family history, trade unions are significant in two early chapters and to a much lesser extent in later chapters. In recent decades, the membership of British trade unions has declined and the structure has changed. Many readers may be unacquainted with these institutions. Therefore, this short note has been composed as an introduction to trade unions for those who are unfamiliar with them.

British trade unions emerged in the 1800s from industrialisation and grew in numbers and strength before some decline occurred at the end of the 1900s. They were created when workers in different sectors of employment joined together to improve pay and conditions at work. Trade unions have long varied in shape and size with many differences between them. One of these has been between the blue collar unions and the white collar unions. The blue collar unions were for manual employees and the white collar unions were for clerical, managerial and professional employees. Of the blue collar unions, some were largely for skilled workers (who had served an apprenticeship), other unions were mainly for workers who were semi-skilled or unskilled. Some unions had members in different sectors of employment; others were for employees in one industry.

Trade unions are organised into branches for similar jobs or a local area and they elect from their number, individuals who are willing to represent their concerns to employers. These voluntary representatives are called shop stewards or lay officials.

In addition to the lay officials, unions employ paid officers (elected or appointed) to support negotiations with employers on behalf of members. The officers help to run the union and organise in new workplaces. Trade unions also employ staff to fulfil tasks such as research, campaigning, finance, and administration. The funding of trade unions is from the subscriptions that are paid by members.

All unions have a national committee (often called an executive) and a general secretary (who is a paid officer). Together they lead the union. Both the executive and the general secretary are elected by individual union members. Each union holds regular conferences, attended by representatives from branches. These conferences decide on the unions priorities. As democratic bodes, strong divisions of opinion are common within a trade union and between it and other trade unions.

Trade unions have constitutions which prescribe the rules by which they are governed. Trade unions are legal entities and if they fail to comply with the law, they can be penalised. Therefore, they are accountable to the wider society to which they belong.

In some sectors of employment, trade unions got together to advance their common interest in negotiations with employers. They formed federations or confederations that appointed representatives to joint councils through which collective bargaining was conducted. Additionally, very early on in their history, at local level in many parts of the country, branches of unions formed associations known as trades councils or trade union councils. Trades union councils bring together unions to work and campaign around issues affecting working people in their local workplaces and communities.

The most important federation in the trade union world is the Trades Union Congress or TUC. Several trade unions formed it in 1868. It was established to be the voice of the unions. Its mission has always been to stand up for working men and women and to make sure their voices are heard. The TUC is the body to which most trade unions in Britain are affiliated. The decision-making body of the TUC is annual congress. At congress, delegates from affiliated unions elect the general council. Delegates are proportionate to union size. Many of the affiliates to the TUC are also affiliated to the Labour party. Between congresses, the general council meets monthly to implement and develop policy, manage TUC financial affairs and deal with any urgent business.

Each year, congress elects a president for the rest of the year who then presides over the congress at the end of the year. The TUC has a permanent staff and the general secretary is its leading figure. The president and the general secretary work closely together.

The TUC campaigns for policy changes that it considers are in the interests of working people. Its lead in policy is decided with the involvement of affiliates. It exercises its influence through discussions with employers, government, political parties and other institutions.

In Scotland there is an independent autonomous body, the Scottish Trades Union Congress or STUC. The STUC represents trade unions with a membership in Scotland and its role north of the border, mirrors that of the TUC.

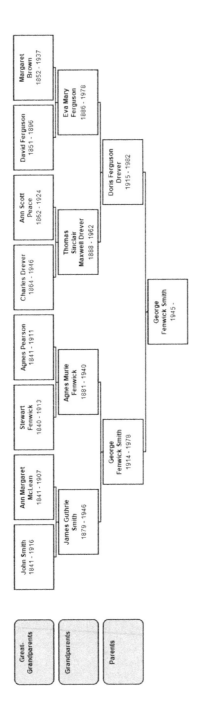

| Great-Grandparents | Grandparents | Parents |

John Smith
1841 - 1916

Ann Margaret McLean
1841 - 1907

Stewart Fenwick
1840 - 1913

Agnes Pearson
1841 - 1911

Charles Drever
1864 - 1946

Ann Scott Peace
1862 - 1924

David Ferguson
1851 - 1896

Margaret Brown
1852 - 1937

James Guthrie Smith
1879 - 1946

Agnes Murie Fenwick
1881 - 1940

Thomas Sinclair Maxwell Drever
1888 - 1962

Eva Mary Ferguson
1886 - 1978

George Fenwick Smith
1914 - 1978

Doris Ferguson Drever
1915 - 1982

George Fenwick Smith
1945 -

Chapter 1

George and Doris
From Dundee to Manchester

This chapter describes the lives of George Fenwick Smith and Doris Ferguson Drever. The chapter encompasses their early years in Dundee where they married in 1937, George's active membership of the Amalgamated Society of Woodworkers (ASW), the war years and George's time as a national organiser in the ASW. George's election as assistant general secretary in the ASW in 1949 and the years that followed in Manchester are described. George's early support for the Independent Labour Party (ILP), then the Communist party and finally the Labour party are explained. The chapter closes with the move of George and Doris to London and the election of George as general secretary of the ASW.

George was a twenty three old journeyman joiner and Doris was a twenty two year old draper's assistant when they married in Dundee in 1937. They became the parents of three children in seven years and their marriage united the eight separate lines of family history that are described in subsequent chapters. The marriage was in the Church of Scotland, both groom and bride having Presbyterian backgrounds. George and Doris were both inhabitants of Dundee and lived in their parental homes. Their fathers were semi-skilled manual workers and their mothers had given up paid manual employment to be full-time mothers and housewives after the birth of the first child in their respective families.

George was the youngest of four siblings and Doris was the eldest of three siblings. At the time of their marriage, Dundee was a city that was still recovering from the Great Depression. A place primarily for the manufacture of jute, the raw material imported from overseas; the industry was at an early stage of decline.

George was born in 1914 in Arbroath, a small industrial town, sixteen miles east of Dundee and situated where the river Tay meets the North Sea. His parents left for Dundee in 1922 when his father, a clicker in the boot and shoe industry, was made unemployed. George, like his father was a red licthtie – the name given to the natives of Arbroath. George's mother was Dundee-born although her family originated from Perthshire. On leaving Arbroath, George's family settled in Downfield, only lately designated as within the Dundee city limits, and therefore not yet an outer suburb but still in character, a village in rural Angus, (the county that surrounded the city). His early years in both these small communities were happy, and as an adult he recalled the virtues of the 'sma' toon' where people knew one another well and trusted each other. George felt that there was a mutual acceptance and plain dealing by people in a 'sma' toon'.

Doris was born in Dundee in 1915. She was, like her mother, a Dundonian by birth and her maternal forebears for several hundred years had inhabited Broughty Ferry, formerly a fishing village in Angus and lately a suburb of Dundee. In contrast, her father was born in the Orkney islands from where his family had migrated to Dundee. Doris's father was a printer's machineman with a local Dundee newspaper. When Doris left school in 1929, she found work as a sales assistant in a departmental store, Smith & Horners, where she worked in the drapery department. It was a job that she liked from the contact it gave her with the public and from her interest in clothes and in having a well presented appearance. Her employment after leaving school was not typical of young women in Dundee, for the principal source of employment for females had long been the jute industry that dominated the local economy. However, the growth of the tertiary sector of the economy in Dundee between the wars created new opportunities and aspirations among females entering the labour market. Shop work was popular among 'respectable' working class girls. The wages and conditions were often more favourable than those of the mills and factories and it was cleaner work but the working hours were also very long. Shop work was seen as the type of job a girl would do before marriage when she would give it up in favour of becoming a full-time housewife.

Whilst Doris was working at Smith and Horners she met George's brother, Stewart, who worked nearby in the Coop store. Through him she met his younger brother George and they began courting. Their courtship included dancing and excursions to the countryside around Dundee in George's motor cycle and sidecar. George earned his living as a joiner. He had worked for a few months in a jute mill when he had left Downfield school in 1928 but did not like the work and left to start an apprenticeship as a joiner and carpenter. He served his five year apprenticeship, with James R. Duncan & Son, a joinery and shopfitting firm in Downfield and he kept warm memories of the experience. He learned how to exercise a wide variety of skills and to handle a wide variety of tools. Being left-handed, he learned to become ambidextrous because some tools were made for right-handers. In November 1933, on completion of his apprenticeship and at the earliest opportunity to do so, he joined the trade union that represented his craft - the ASW.

George was to remain a member of the ASW and its successor, the Union of Construction, Allied Trades and Technicians (UCATT), for the rest of his life. It became the main arbiter of his life. As a journeyman joiner he was a craftsman who could expect a wage to match the skills that he possessed. However, Dundee had been badly hit by the Great Depression and in 1933, there was a level of unemployment which in reality but not formally, was 70% and therefore amongst the highest in the country. There being no vacancies for journeymen joiners in Dundee, George left with a peer to find work in London. They found lodgings in Hammersmith and their earnings were sufficient to pay for occasional admission to the Hammersmith Palais. Before long, they returned to Dundee where there was renewed activity in the building trade and George found employment in shop fitting. Improvements and extensions of premises in the business centre were taking place and modern frontages were being created for shops.

George's employment in his early years in the trade was as a travelling journeyman. Employment was casual in the building trade so the journeyman was paid by the hour. Men could be taken on and sacked at an hour's notice. Equally, a man who had started work but disliked what he was doing could leave almost immediately. The trade offered little security but it did offer freedom. In the practice of his trade, George began to acquire and keep a store of tools which became a great treasury that he still possessed at the end of his life. He expected of himself, a high standard of craftsmanship and was able to perform a wide range of woodworking tasks, taking great pride in his work.

Doris discovered early in her courtship with George that his work as a joiner was complemented by politics and trade unionism. He and his siblings had been brought up in household that talked trade unionism and socialism from childhood. His father was a keen trade unionist and strong supporter of the ILP and his mother had a paternal family history of religious and political dissent in Perthshire.

George was active in the Independent Labour Party. For some years it had been politically influential in the city after the formation of a branch in the city in 1893. Its municipal candidates had enjoyed electoral success. However, after national disaffiliation from the Labour Party in 1932 because of policy disagreement, and now distinctly to its Left, the ILP began to decline in Dundee. After 1932 few individuals stood as ILP municipal candidates and they attracted little electoral support. Disregarding its declining support,

George remained a member and was involved in sending aid to the Republican side in the Spanish Civil War. There was considerable effort organised in Dundee to do this between 1936 and 1939 by the Labour Movement as a whole. George also campaigned for the party by standing on a soapbox in Dundee and proclaiming the policies of the ILP to any passing citizens who were interested.

George's political commitment was inspired by his father's unswerving support for the ILP and by the conspicuously poor inter-war living conditions of Dundee. Because of the decline of the jute industry, unemployment remained extensive and housing too was marked by high levels of overcrowding. Dundee in fact was recognised as a Scottish leader in urban squalor. The poet Hugh MacDiarmid on visiting Dundee at this time described the city as a grim monument of man's inhumanity to man. For George, the ILP offered an answer to these problems although the Communist party (founded in 1920), began to replace the declining ILP after 1932. Although it did not achieve electoral success in the city, the Communist party commanded much support because it offered an unqualified defence of the unemployed. It sponsored the National Unemployed Workers Movement that drew public notice to the plight of the unemployed by means of demonstrations. Bob Stewart was the most prominent communist in the city between the wars and served the party at national level also. He was a colourful character with a record of imprisonment for his political activities. The sturdy support for the Communist party in the city was shown, for example, by the vote of over ten thousand for Bob Stewart at the 1931 general election and by the meeting in the city in January 1938 addressed by Harry Pollitt (general secretary of the Communist party) which drew two thousand people.

From his membership of the ASW, George was elected to various offices in his branch (Dundee third). These branch responsibilities gave him experience, confidence and satisfaction. He developed aspirations for exerting greater political influence both for members and for working class people generally. Doris was told by him that one day that he would be general secretary of the ASW. George was elected by his branch as its representative on the Dundee district management committee of the ASW. This body coordinated the activities of branches in its area. From the management committee he became a delegate to the National Federation of Building Trade Operatives – the federation of trade unions active in the building industry.

After Doris and George married, because of their limited housing options, they moved in with his parents and later her parents. Their first child, Eva was born in January 1938. They later secured a tenancy in a four storey tenement.

Changes in the economy occurred in anticipation of war with Germany, one of which was a contraction of non-essential work and an expansion of work that contributed to the war effort. In Dundee, work for shopfitting dried up but the Caledon shipyard, offered plenty of work and so George joined the labour force of three thousand and five hundred. War was declared on Germany in September 1939 and the Caledon yard's many trades were at full stretch throughout the war. They were engaged in making frigates, corvettes, seven standard "B" type tramps, four fast cargo-liners, three fleet refuellers along with private merchant orders. They also carried out repairs to over one thousand ships including many destroyers and submarines. An aircraft carrier was launched from the yard in 1942.

George was conscripted for military service early in the War but was exempted because he was in a reserved occupation. The reserved (or scheduled) occupation scheme was a complicated one, covering five million men in a vast range of jobs. Those in reserved occupations were key skilled workers and the age range varied for occupation. The reserved occupations were often far from a soft option. Hours were long and conditions often difficult. The government was determined not to repeat the mistakes of World War One, when the indiscriminate recruitment of too many men into the military had left major war production schemes short of the necessary workforce. It kept the scheme under review and later in the War George lost his exemption, was again conscripted and again exempted because he was unfit through having a duodenal ulcer. Doris had to spend much time in queueing up to buy suitable food for his digestive ailment. The family increased in size in 1941 when a son, Eric was born. During the war, the inhabitants of Dundee were exposed to the dangers of enemy bombing but only very slightly compared to other British cities. There were one hundred and thirty two red alerts in Dundee between October 1939 and April 1944 and there was damage, deaths and injuries from the thirty eight bombs that fell within the city boundary.

During the war, George was elected to various offices on the Dundee district management committee of the ASW. From there, he became a delegate to the Confederation of Shipbuilding and Engineering Unions, the body that brought together all the trade unions in that industry. In 1942 he was elected secretary of the district management committee. He was also a trade union representative on the Local Appeals Board set up in wartime for workers dismissed at the Shipyard.

At the Caledon shipyard, George became a member of the yard committee. This was a joint production committee formed to bring management and worker representatives together to improve production and hasten victory in the War. The Communist party was enthusiastically in favour of these bodies to support the war effort and thereby lend succour to the Soviet Union after it had been invaded in 1941. As such, it was also hostile to unofficial strikes taking place. These committees were first established in 1941 and then became more widely adopted throughout the engineering and allied industries in 1942 after a national agreement between the unions and employers. Chaired by a senior manager, they comprised a maximum of ten representatives from each side of industry who met monthly. Their discussions at times extended beyond their brief to wages and welfare. The workers' representatives were shop stewards who were elected by their members. The joint production committees educated workers in the problems of management and educated management in the problems of workers. They have been credited with having harnessed the knowledge and experience of working men and women to increase output. George's membership of the joint production committee suggests that he gained much experience in representing his members, negotiating on their behalf and collaborating with other trade unions.

Whilst he was at the Caledon shipyard, George transferred his political allegiance from the ILP to the Communist party. It was only a short ideological step to do this and many others before him had taken the same step. Exactly when George did this is a secret but the historical context suggests that it was around 1942, the year when public support for the Communist party peaked in Britain with membership reaching an all-time high of fifty six thousand. By this time George had been persuaded to support the party by John Brown, party member, engineering worker and leading shop steward on the yard committee. Brown later held full-time office in his own union. The ILP had seriously declined by now whereas the Communist party was on the rise and offered a prospectus that mirrored George's own beliefs about the need for fundamental change in Britain to redress the exploitation of working class people. George's membership of the Communist party led to his acquaintance with Dave Bowman, (later President of the National Union of Railwaymen) to whom the baton of communist leadership in the city had been passed by Bob Stewart.

In addition to his work at the shipyard, at home, George volunteered as an Air Raid Precautions (ARP) warden of which there were eight hundred in Dundee during World War Two. The ARP (renamed Civil Defence in September 1941) was locally based so the wardens knew their sector and the people living there in the event of air raids. The wardens were supposed to be on duty about three nights a week and they enforced the blackout, and fitted the civilian population in Dundee with gas masks amongst other duties. They were given training, helmets, uniforms and equipment. One duty that George frequently performed was fire watching from the roof of a building. As a warden, his time for sleep was reduced but he was still required to put in a full day's work at the shipyard. All the wardens such as George relinquished their duties when Civil defence was disbanded late in 1944.

The end of the war in 1945 brought two particular changes for the Smith family. The family was enlarged by the birth of a third child, George, junior and later in the year, George, senior, was appointed as national organiser of the ASW in Scotland. He became a full-time officer of the union instead of a lay official. The ASW members at the Caledon shipyard showed their appreciation of George's service to them by making him a gift of a traveller's wallet and a fountain pen which was presented at the quarterly meeting of the Dundee and district shop stewards in June. The post that George held as national organiser for Scotland was one of nine new ASW appointments, responsible for those areas of Britain, usually small towns and rural areas, where the union was poorly organised. In his new post, George travelled by public transport from his home in Dundee, all over Scotland, including the Highlands and the islands.

Amongst George's new responsibilities was assisting ASW members working at the new dam that was being built at Pitlochry, Perthshire as part of the larger Tummel-Garry Hydro-Electric Scheme intended to bring electricity to the Highlands. For the vast majority of the workers on the scheme the pay was high but they mostly lived in temporary work camps nearby the construction sites. These were tough places to live with food and accommodation of variable quality. Off duty there was little for the workers to do but drink. Alcohol-fuelled fights were commonplace, with the police called to restore peace regularly. The low regard for health and safety issues led to a high accident rate and deaths among the workers. There was considerable local opposition to the scheme at Pitlochry and employees of the Scheme were ostracised and refused accommodation from fear that the works would blight the scenery and drive away visitors. Pitlochry was a small remote village with few facilities. Many of the workers at Pitlochry had been recruited from Dundee. At the start of the works in 1947, there was severe weather and in the autumn, heavy rain caused much damage to the project including the collapse of a river bank, a crane and a derrick. To recover the lost ground, the workers had to work for a spell in constant shifts in heavy rain without time off. In January, 1948 after enduring a Spartan experience of working on the dam, the labour force comprising different trades was threatened with the withdrawal of free refreshments at their breaks. The two hundred and fifty men working for the contractor George Wimpey went on strike. The dispute was settled a few days later. As a national organiser, George was a regular visitor to Pitlochry to assist ASW members.

George's post as a national organiser was in a trade union that was highly decentralised with much local autonomy. In places with several branches in close geographical proximity, district management committees were elected which co-ordinated the activities of the branches, appointed full-time officials and made local policy for their areas. In other places, branches that were isolated struggled to fulfil all their functions. There was an uneven pattern of organisation with the union well organised and strong in urban industrial areas, but in small towns and rural areas, it lacked resources and strength. The ASW resembled a mosaic of parishes for it was still largely based around local collective bargaining. However, national agreements had superseded local deals in 1918 and had become ever more important. This was demonstrated by the national agreement of 1947 that legitimised payment by results in the building industry that hitherto, had relied on payment by the hour. The agreement ultimately had a massive impact for all localities.

Post-war demands were made by some branches of the ASW for organisational reform that prompted a debate. George sided with those who were calling for structural change. His experience as national organiser acquainted him with the union in settings that were differed from that of Dundee and district with which he was familiar. He came to see the union as primitive and lopsided in its organisational development and therefore failing to make an even impact throughout the country. He urged support for a national conference (before its inauguration in 1947) and for re-organisation of the union into regions and defined districts with periodic delegate conferences. Essentially, he believed that the highly decentralised structure of the ASW, largely unchanged from its earliest years, was no longer fit for purpose. Greater centralisation was necessary to make the union stronger throughout the whole country. A more considered set of arrangements and uniform distribution of resources geographically were required. He opined to members that the organisation of the union resulted in it occupying a disgraceful position of mediocrity in the trade union and labour movement. In putting his oar in, George placed himself at odds with the general secretary, Frank Wolstencroft, who defended the highly decentralised status quo. Nonetheless, George felt that reform would secure a more soundly based and properly run union that would keep it strong and intact. In subsequent years, he maintained his support for greater centralisation and was eventually able to engineer it when the ASW merged with other unions to become UCATT.

In 1948, the retirement of Frank Wolstencroft from the post of general secretary prompted an election in which George was a candidate. He was defeated by the successful candidate, Jack McDermott. McDermott had served as a member of the executive council (the governing body of the ASW), and subsequently as assistant general secretary so he was well known to members throughout the whole country. McDermott vacated the post of assistant general secretary for which an election was held in 1949. George was one of the twenty three candidates that were nominated. After a prolonged election process comprising several distinct stages, George was elected with a large majority over his two rivals.

George vacated the post of national organiser and prepared to migrate to Manchester where the assistant general secretary was based in the headquarters of the ASW. Whilst Doris and George expected the move to provide better opportunities for the three children later in their lives, Doris anticipated with regret, distant separation from her family in Dundee. However, to offset that separation, there were regular family visits to Dundee. The move to Manchester provided the family with an improvement in accommodation. In leaving Dundee they left a fourth floor inner city Victorian tenement that comprised a kitchen/living room with box bed, Victorian cooking range, cold water tap, and two other rooms. The toilet was shared on the landing and the movable zinc bath was used in the living room with water boiled on the range. In the Manchester suburb of Withington, the family lived in a terraced house with scullery, two sitting rooms, three bedrooms and a separate toilet and bathroom. There were also small gardens front and rear and a wash house at the rear.

George was elected as a senior officer of the ASW at a time when a climate of hostility had developed in the trade union movement towards officials who were members of the Communist party. The Cold War prompted the belief that the Communist party was a direct instrument of Soviet policy and it therefore constituted a danger to national security. The climate of hostility was shown in 1948 when the general council of the Trades Union Congress (TUC) issued a document titled *Defend Democracy* that urged unions to consider banning communists from holding union posts and acting as union delegates. In 1949, the largest TUC affiliate, the Transport and General Workers Union, voted to ban communists from holding office. Nine full-time officials were dismissed. Strong anti-communist currents emerged in unions where communists were active. The ASW was not immune to this climate of suspicion and hostility towards communists and therefore neither was George. In 1950, the communist *Daily Worker* newspaper had reported in a triumphalist way that of the six delegates elected by the ASW to the TUC annual congress, four were Communist party members. The general secretary, Jack McDermott opined to members that when the delegates were elected, their party affiliations were not known and that communist candidates elected to union office accepted the dictation of an outside body which was not acceptable. Hostility to communists in the union was led Norman Kennedy, an erstwhile communist and a member of the executive council, from 1949 until his death in a road accident in 1954.

George was a member of the ASW delegation to the annual congress of the Scottish TUC in 1952. The event had a personal significance for him because the delegation helped to pass a resolution to boycott the publications of D.C. Thomson & Co as a result of its dismissal of employees who were trade unionists. George was fully in support of the STUC decision although his father-in-law, as a long-serving employee of D.C.Thomson & Co, theoretically, now had his job put at risk.

As assistant general secretary, George had in effect, a three year contract, for the post was subject to regular election. In 1953, he was re-elected with a large majority over the other nineteen candidates. Later that year and perhaps encouraged by his re-election, he decided to challenge the executive council over a decision that it had made, to which he took exception. The general secretary was on sick leave and the executive council decided to appoint as acting general secretary, one of its long-serving members, Sam McKelvey. George felt that this decision was not merely a slight to his integrity and competence; it was also a contravention of the union rules. Not only had the five full-time member executive council snubbed him, they had breached union rules. He felt that it had exceeded its authority at his expense and he was determined that the decision should be aborted. He decided to object to the decision, whatever the consequences. At his instigation, a special meeting of the general council of the ASW was held in July. The general council comprised nine lay members who heard appeals against the decisions of the executive council. The general council determined that within the union's rules, the executive council was not entitled to appoint McKelvey, nor was McKelvey entitled to be acting general secretary. It therefore rescinded the decision of the executive council to appoint him as such. The decision of the general council was a strong rebuke to the executive council. It enhanced George's standing for it suggested that in the absence of the general secretary, George was his deputy. Moreover, it suggested that George was a trustworthy servant of the union who acted in full compliance with its rules. The incident also demonstrated George's traits that his acquaintances knew well. He was a determined, forceful, and ambitious character.

In 1954, George broke with his past by leaving the Communist party. Two years later, many others did likewise but for a different reason. They were appalled by the Soviet Union suppressing the Hungarian uprising. George's departure preceded that international event and was the culmination of his increasing disenchantment with the party. When he had joined it as a shipyard shop steward in war-time, it had offered a comfortable home to him. Since then, as a full-time trade union official, his experience had been greatly extended. From that experience, he had concluded that communist dogma did not have much to do with the realities of trade unionism. He had come to feel that the Communist party was a purveyor of shibboleths, principal of which was the notion of the proletariat. The concept of the proletariat suggested a working class that exhibited solidarity from which a new social order would be created. George's trade union experience suggested that the working class was not a wholly united and cohesive stratum that was intent on a society-wide change. He found that working class solidarity was strongly tempered by instrumentality so that trade unionists firstly sought improvement for their particular trade or occupation. Broader schemes for social improvement were of secondary importance to most trade unionists, he inferred.

George's change of political outlook was much influenced by his experience of the members of the ASW who he recognised as silver arsed craftsmen. As such, they expected their union to secure recognition for them commensurate with their status and differentiated them from workers with lesser skills. Still wishing to participate in political change, George followed the path of many ex-communists and joined the Labour party as it was now more in keeping with his revised outlook. He maintained his belief in the pursuit of social equality but he concluded that the removal of class barriers required a more flexible and gradualist strategy that would address a complex and evolving society. He remained a socialist who still valued the principle, 'from each according to his ability, to each according to his needs'. In relinquishing his membership of the Communist party, George never became as others did who left the party, an anti-communist He was willing to collaborate with communists or others with different ideological leanings, where they shared common ground with him. Later on in his life, as a member of the general council of the TUC, he found himself in the company of other union officials who had followed a political path like his own.

Although in 1954 George revised his political affiliations, in his personal life, he upheld traditional gender divisions. Eldest daughter, Eva, had stayed at school beyond the compulsory school leaving to sixteen and her educational attainment and aspirations suggested progression to higher education. To George, there were adverse financial implications from bearing the cost of Eva's further educational progression and he vetoed it. To ameliorate the adverse financial implications, Doris expressed her willingness to return to paid work but George's objection persisted because he feared the family overall would lose if Doris returned to work. Eva's aspiration for higher education was postponed until her adulthood.

As assistant general secretary, George had little opportunity to change the organisation of the ASW although he retained his belief that the structure of the union was outmoded. His belief was supported by his acquaintance with a working class intellectual, Vic Allen. Allen, a bricklayer turned academic, published his PhD, *Power in Trade Unions*, in 1954. His study was greatly facilitated by the cooperation that the ASW gave him. Allen's analysis suggested that the ASW's structure had remained largely intact since its adoption by the founder of the union, Robert Applegarth, in the Victorian age. Years later, Allen's reputation was tarnished by his unwavering support for Stalinist communism. Allen's study supported George's belief that the ASW required organisational updating. He drew his own conclusions from this study, just as he did from many other sources that he consulted, both practical and academic, throughout his life. Since leaving school, aged fourteen, George had learned much from his life experience and from people, events, and the printed word in its various forms. He was consistently interested in uniting theory with practice and accordingly was receptive to individuals who possessed theoretical expertise. Another working class intellectual who influenced his thinking was Tom Connelly, who was the research officer of the ASW for several years. His history of the union was published in 1960 and he later enjoyed a career in public administration that culminated in appointment as the first chief executive of the Commission for Racial Equality.

Soon after George had joined the Labour Party, Hugh Gaitskell became its leader in 1955 and he became a strong supporter of Gaitskell's political leadership. Gaitskell had addressed the annual conference of the ASW in 1955 and George had been impressed. He believed that Gaitskell was in touch with political realities in contrast to his critics on the Left who purveyed political shibboleths. Gaitskell's appeal to George was both in terms of the man's qualities and his political message. Gaitskell was a conviction politician, a man of integrity with strong beliefs which he courageously propounded. He upheld economic planning, collectivism, Keynesianism to sustain full employment, multilateral disarmament, and the pursuit of economic and social equality. George shared the same ideas as Gaitskell.

In 1956, George was again re-elected as assistant general secretary. He had a bigger majority over the other six candidates than in his election in 1953. The following year, 1957, an upheaval for him and the family occurred when the headquarters of the ASW moved from Manchester to London to make it easier for representation in the centre of trade union affairs. From 1958, their new home in Croydon was a further improvement in housing conditions for it was a link-detached house with three bedroom, two sitting rooms, kitchen, toilet and bathroom, with garage and generous sized gardens to front and rear.

In 1958, Jack McDermott was re-elected as general secretary but his time in the post was short lived for he died of cancer before the end of the year. The electoral process for assistant general secretary had started before his death and the outcome was George's re-election with a large majority over the other eighteen candidates. The vacancy for general secretary triggered an election for which George became a candidate. He could demonstrate a record of good service to the union nationally from his ten years as assistant general secretary. Only one candidate believed he could successfully challenge George for the post and in the event, George secured a very large majority over him. In the subsequent periodic elections for the post of general secretary of the ASW (and its successor UCATT), George was elected on each occasion with a large majority. The remainder of the lives of George and Doris in London after his election as general secretary are described in chapter 2.

Chapter 2

George and Doris
The TUC years

This chapter describes the lives of George and Doris after his election in 1959 as general secretary of the Amalgamated Society of Woodworkers (ASW). It includes George's election to the general council of the TUC, of which he remained a member until his death; his quest for union reform that culminated in the formation of the Union of Construction and Allied Trades and Technicians (UCATT); his period of alcoholism and recovery; his years as general secretary of UCATT; the 1972 building industry strike; his support for the Labour government's Social Contract. The chapter closes with the deaths of George and Doris in 1978 and 1982 respectively.

On his election as general secretary of the ASW in 1959, George became the CEO of a trade union with a membership of one hundred and eighty seven thousand spread over several industries; more than two thirds in building and civil engineering. The union had a long history from the amalgamation in 1922 of two unions and a family tree originating in local trade clubs that combined in 1827. One of his predecessors as general secretary, Robert Applegarth, had a distinguished record. He had made the union a significant force and was an influential propagandist for trade unions from 1862 to 1871. By pure chance, George's home in Croydon was one mile from Robert Applegarth's home in retirement. As general secretary, George acquired several major responsibilities. He now represented the ASW in negotiations with employers in the building industry. He represented the ASW at the TUC and managed its relations with the Labour Party. Overall, he was the custodian of the ASW, charged with securing its future.

On the National Joint Council for the building industry, George became a member of the operatives' side. The union side was constituted by representatives from the different trades. As the ASW had the largest membership in the industry, its general secretary had a big say. Through the National Joint Council, the trade unions met the employers regularly to negotiate wages and conditions nationally. The ASW, with all the other trade unions in the building industry shared a problem that was intrinsic to the industry. The industry had a high labour mobility and given that much employment was casual, workers did not have the same continuous employment or trade union attachment as in other industries. Building sites were temporary and geographically dispersed, and controlled by different employers and sub-contractors. Trade union organisation was difficult in the industry. Trade unionism in the industry was seriously undermined by the growth of labour only sub-contracting and self-employment. Although it had a long history, tax changes in1966 and thereafter strongly encouraged labour only sub-contracting. Many self-employed preferred to negotiate directly with main and specialist subcontractors and union membership proved of little advantage to them. Many workers decided that there were considerable financial advantages for them in being self-employed and downgraded the risks that they faced from this form of employment. Gangs of labour-only sub-contractors came to be hired in the industry. Negotiations with the employers were not easy and in 1963 limited strikes at selected sites were deployed before a settlement could be reached.

One particular problem that confronted George in the building industry was unofficial activity at site level. This was shown by disputes at the Barbican and Horseferry Road in 1967. The report of the court of inquiry chaired by Lord Cameron into the prolonged stoppages at Horseferry Road and the Barbican was critical of a lack of supervision and control by the unions in construction over site committees. The Cameron report referred to the subversive and mischievous influence of unofficial joint union committees. After, the report was published, George and the other building union leaders placed an advertisement in newspapers urging that unofficial activities cease at the Barbican site. George thought that these events tarnished the reputation of trade unions and that ultimately they might be damaged by them. He and the executive committee of the ASW instructed branches not to support unofficial stoppages or unofficial shop stewards committees.

In 1959, George led his union delegation for the first time to the annual congress of the Trade Union Congress. At the TUC, delegates from across Britain gathered to decide policy. The governing body between annual congresses was the general council and George was elected to it. In the years that followed, his annual re-election resulted in him becoming 'father' of the council or longest serving member on his death in 1978. As a member of the inner circle of the TUC, he was appointed to several of its committees, including, the economic committee. The TUC brought him into regular contact with many other union leaders. It also extended his acquaintance with politicians, senior civil servants and other policy makers. In 1960, George Woodcock was elected general secretary of the TUC. Woodcock had a distinct philosophy of trade unionism that reverberated with George's own developing outlook. The view that both shared maintained that trade unions had a moral responsibility to contribute to public policy that was generally beneficial and not merely to only pursue their own sectional interest. The premise of this view was that governments since the Second World War had accepted a responsibility, that they had hitherto eschewed, for management of the economy, including full employment. If they were to succeed in the exercise of these responsibilities, they required the support of trade unions and responsible conduct on their part. That might include restraint and changes in structure and practices. If trade unions failed to act in a responsible manner, in the democratic age, they would he held to account by public opinion and ultimately their political influence would be curbed. Many union leaders did not share Woodcock's view but George did and it informed his conduct as a trade union leader until his death. He also believed that trade unions had a responsibility to support working class friendly governments which he later demonstrated most conspicuously by his support for the Social Contract.

George's support for socially responsible trade unionism was expressed immediately on becoming general secretary. In 1959, he informed members that in a free society the management of full employment without inflation required recognition by trade unionists that wage policies had an important contribution to make. A Labour government would only make progress if trade unions played their part in helping through wages policies. He reiterated this view on many subsequent occasions and asserted that Labour governments depended on trade union support and cooperation to pursue social justice. That cooperation required trade unions to accept some restraints and restrictions on freedom of action. Without that patient cooperation, a Labour government might founder. He later expressed his support for co-ordination in wage bargaining as necessary for a Labour government to secure its economic and social goals. He came to accept the need for an incomes policy, which should include restraints on prices and higher incomes and ideally should be pursued through the TUC and on a voluntary basis. George admired the centralised bargaining between employers and trade unions in other Western European countries such as Sweden and West Germany, for it was in keeping with his belief in the benefits from centralisation of trade unions. Throughout his life he consistently argued for centralisation of trade unions and his last public support for it was expressed in a motion in conjunction with restructuring, at the annual congress of the TUC in 1977. Of the Labour government's proposals for industrial relations made in 1969, he observed that the majority were acceptable with only a minority that could be opposed by trade unions. He cautioned against trade unions undermining the Labour government lest they had to confront a different government that was much more committed to the control of trade union power. The cabinet minister, Barbara Castle, noticed that he was one of only two TUC leaders who expressed their appreciation to her for the government abandoning its proposals for reform of industrial relations.

In fulfilling his trade union responsibilities, George was taken to a wider world. In 1965 he was appointed as the representative of the TUC on the National Committee for Commonwealth Immigrants. The National Committee for Commonwealth Immigrants (NCCI) was formed by the Home Secretary in September 1965 as a result of the white paper of that year on immigration from the commonwealth. Its chairman was the Archbishop of Canterbury, and it was tasked with promoting and co-ordinating on a national basis efforts directed towards the integration of commonwealth immigrants into the community. The NCCI was itself succeeded by the Community Relations Commission (CRC) in 1968. George was next appointed by the Government to the Committee on Immigration Appeals chaired by Sir Roy Wilson. The report of the committee led to legislation that introduced a system of immigration appeals in 1969. George was made a Commander of the British Empire in the Queen's Birthday Honours of June 1969. He was proud to accept this honour because it was awarded by a Labour government. Had the honour been conferred by a Conservative government he would have declined because he believed that the Conservative party was intrinsically opposed to the interests of working class people.

In the same year as the award of his honour, George, accompanied by Doris, represented the TUC at the convention in Miami of the equivalent of the TUC in the United States, the AFL-CIO. Two years earlier, he was appointed to the Board of the Commonwealth Development Corporation. The CDC had been established in 1948 to augment the productive capacity of the colonies to provide food and raw materials to meet the pressing needs of post-war Britain. It was oriented towards investing in public sector projects. In subsequent years it evolved its development role towards the raising of living standards in poor commonwealth countries. George was appointed to bring a trade union perspective to the decision-making of the Board.

On his election as general secretary, George expressed strong support for the Labour Party which he urged upon his members. He expressed his beliefs in democratic socialism, which for him included the need for compromise. He continued to express his support for the Labour party when it was in opposition and in government. In 1959, he blamed the Conservative government for the prevailing economic problems and foresaw an improvement by its replacement with a Labour government. Within the Labour party he associated the ASW with Gaitskell's leadership when he moved a resolution at the annual Labour Party conference at Scarborough in 1960 that supported multilateral disarmament. The motion was consistent with the defence policy that Gaitskell advocated and although it was defeated, unilateralism was renounced at the annual conference in 1961. George was amongst the TUC general council members who informally met together in support of Gaitskell's leadership. They met for dinner before meetings of the general council. When Gaitskell died prematurely in 1963, George felt that there was a serious loss for the Labour Party. The Labour leaders that succeeded him never secured the admiration that he had felt for Gaitskell.

George was not silent when he felt critical of the Labour party in or out of office. When the Prices and Incomes Board reduced a pay rise in the construction industry by a tiny amount in 1969, George was critical. The cabinet minister and diarist, Barbara Castle, was alarmed by the 'violent noises' that she heard from him but the full pay rise was eventually conceded, conditional on productivity strings. Barbara Castle considered him to be a 'worthwhile chap'.

Soon after his election as general secretary, George identified the drop in membership as a serious matter confronting the ASW and it exercised his mind in the years that followed. The membership of the ASW had fallen from a peak of two hundred and one thousand, three hundred in 1947. To him, the persisting decline in membership had to be stemmed or the union would lose its influence. He contended that structural change was necessary to reverse the decline with a modification of the highly decentralised structure. He believed that the exercise of local autonomy in the ASW was achieved at the cost of a loss of efficiency in organisational resources. He asserted that a more effective structure was required to raise membership and improve services to members. He proposed larger organising areas and greater direction of organising resources. He re-iterated his support for organisational change and specifically proposed the replacement of district structures by regional structures including a shift from annual conferences to biennial conferences supplemented by regional conferences. However, only minor alteration of district structures was accepted by the ASW. The reforms in full that he championed were only accepted when major structural changes occurred through amalgamation with other trade unions in 1971.

George's modernising instincts were also encouraged by TUC initiatives to foster re-organisation of affiliated unions. The initiatives showed George Woodcock's belief in the need for trade union reform with which George was in sympathy. He was willing to contemplate extensive organisational change despite his experience of strong resistance to it from within his own union. In 1952 the union had agreed to admit semi-skilled workers and women but in practice the decision was not upheld by all branches which did not encourage recruitment of other than skilled workers. The ASW's conservative outlook to organisational change was also demonstrated at its conference in 1959 when a resolution for one union for the building industry was overwhelmingly rejected. George's belief was that without adapting its organisation to the changing environment, the ASW would decline in membership and influence. He believed that the innate conservatism of craftsmen sometimes resulted in opposition to changes which were virtually inevitable. He concluded that to persuade the silver arsed craftsmen of the ASW to agree to organisational change much persistence and skill was required.

In 1963 George opined that the scope for the ASW to amalgamate with two other woodworking unions was small but there was a greater chance of amalgamation with other unions in the construction industry. The shrewdness of his view was confirmed several years later when negotiations with two other woodworking unions concluded without an agreement and they chose partners other than the ASW. However, George was successful in securing amalgamation with the small National Union of Packing Case Makers in 1965. Negotiations with other unions in the construction industry were conducted but two of them eschewed amalgamation with the ASW for other partners. Eventually, the persisting decline of union membership in construction and concomitant financial losses was the catalyst to a successful outcome from negotiations with several unions. In 1970, the Amalgamated Society of Painters and Decorators, the small Association of Building Technicians and the Amalgamated Union of Building Trade Workers all agreed to merge with the ASW. In 1971 the amalgamated woodworkers, painters, technicians, and bricklayers adopted the title of the Union of Construction, Allied Trades and Technicians, (UCATT), and became the tenth largest union affiliated to the TUC. The new union was open to virtually all workers in construction, irrespective of craft or skill.

The merger was the outcome of a complex period of careful negotiation that was led by George. The new union that emerged was largely shaped by him for there were no other alternative plans offered from any quarter. Moreover, George was the dominant personality in all the discussions that were held. The amalgamation incorporated changes that he had advocated for the ASW long before the merger. George succeeded in structuring UCATT along the lines that he had long espoused with a regional structure displacing district organisation, biennial conferences and a more integrated structure. Power in the new union was concentrated at the centre rather than the periphery. The office of general secretary of the new union was subject to periodic election. In many trade unions, there was an election for the office of general secretary initially, after which the incumbent had permanent tenure until retirement. George believed that whatever other unions did, the CEO of UCATT must be publicly accountable to members through periodic election. He was also confident that he represented his members well and that his service would be recognised at elections as long as he was a candidate for office. George was re-elected comfortably as general secretary of UCATT just as he had been in the ASW.

In the years that immediately followed his election as general secretary of the ASW, George became more reliant on the use of alcohol in his daily life. He had consumed alcohol freely from his early years, just as he had tobacco, and his alcohol addiction became more obvious in the office that he now held with its important responsibilities to fulfil. A gradual change occurred in his behaviour that showed his increasing reliance on alcohol. There were many social events that he attended where alcohol was consumed and informally there were also frequent occasions when this happened also. His drinking patterns were erratic with him sometimes sober, sometimes slightly intoxicated, and sometimes seriously under the influence of alcohol. In general, his increased reliance on alcohol resulted in him being ever more absent from home and therefore unable to fulfil family responsibilities. He was absent for parents evenings at school, for example. For Doris it was a difficult time to cope with his erratic behaviour which she could not understand. There was no domestic violence or ensuing financial difficulties but much tension was generated at home between George and Doris. George's unreliable behaviour was disruptive and provoked Doris to anger on occasions but mostly she maintained a distance from him to display her disapproval. Behind the distance there was silent anger. How George conducted himself at work during the time of his alcohol addiction is a mystery. His reliance on alcohol developed to the point where he turned to a glass of whisky first thing in the morning. His drinking problems in 1963, led to his absence from the annual congress of the TUC and annual conference of the Labour Party.

In 1964 there was some stabilisation in George's behaviour and that was followed by him experiencing a coronary for which he was hospitalised for a few weeks. His visitors in hospital included George Woodcock. For some months his reliance on alcohol abated but normality then slipped away and heavy alcohol consumption returned. In 1965, when all the children had left home, to secure relief from George's alcoholism, Doris stayed for a few weeks at her parents' home in Dundee. In Doris's absence from home, George's drinking took its most serious turn and he was admitted to hospital urgently in a very poor state of health, suffering from malnutrition. He had stopped eating regularly and appropriately in favour of the consumption of alcohol. It was at this point that he started a slow process of recovery. Before this nadir in his life, he had attempted to address his alcoholism through membership of Alcoholics Anonymous. However, the mutual support that it offered proved unsuitable for George because as an atheist, he found the religious premise of the association an obstacle to his recovery. He now became a psychiatric outpatient through which he obtained therapy that enabled him to renounce his dependence on alcohol. The medical treatment he received prompted him to admit he was an alcoholic and consequently to recover from the illness. He was given means other than alcohol to fight his demons. Soon after his renunciation of alcohol, he also abandoned his addiction to nicotine.

In his recovery from alcoholism George made adjustments to his life. Freed of his addiction to alcohol, his recreational interests developed. He bought a camera and took up photography and also reacquainted himself with woodwork for which he had never lost his skills. Ever since being first elected as a union official he had vowed that if he was ever defeated in an election, he would 'return to the tools' – resume his trade as a joiner. That fate never happened but exercising the skills of a craftsman ever appealed to him. He returned to woodwork by constructing a dark room adjacent to the garage at home and fitting it out. He also constructed a workshop in the garden and fitted it suitably with a bench and storage facilities for the tools that had long been in his possession. He later floored the attic at home and fitted it out to become a photographic studio. He started to enjoy listening to classical music on long-playing records that he had bought. A caravan was bought and trips made for breaks, particularly in Scotland. With some cash to spare for the first time in his life, he followed Doris's suggestion of savings regularly through a building society that permitted holidays abroad.

After making the acquaintance of a fellow Scot, Dr Robert Murray, the medical adviser to the TUC, George disclosed to him that he was a recovered alcoholic. Murray had addressed the ASW annual conference in 1967 on occupational health and he recognised the value of the disclosure. He persuaded George to contribute to symposia held by the Medical Council on Alcoholism (as it was then known). The symposia were to educate health professionals in harm reduction from alcoholism and George informed them of his own experience in battling with the illness. Owing to his many more pressing commitments, Murray withdrew from the MCA in 1971, and as a result, George made no further contributions to the symposia.

In the transition from the ASW to UCATT in 1971, George's responsibilities as general secretary remained much the same but became more onerous. For as chief of the new union (and its architect), the onus was on him to establish from the separate parts from which it had been created, a unified and effective body. In the building industry he became secretary of the operatives' side of the national joint council, a pivotal role when negotiations stalled and a strike was called in 1972. By the time he became UCATT general secretary, George was a senior member of the general council of the TUC as a result of his long service. Consequently, his obligations to the TUC increased in importance and by association, to the Labour party too.

The formation of UCATT brought together separate unions that were largely craft in their character, but they were nonetheless different in their histories, structures, budgets, procedures, customs, political allegiances and the personalities of leading officials. As CEO, it was incumbent on George to synthesise all the disparate strands into one united union. The new union inherited dissimilar organisational arrangements and financial difficulties, both of which had to be addressed. Important decisions were made that necessitated economies and rationalisation to make the union strong. Within a few years the union was put on a sound financial and organisational basis. George had to work with a much enlarged executive council, until its membership was reduced over time by retirements. This and other matters demanded careful management by him to secure an effective integrated organisation.

One of the matters that had long concerned George was unofficial activity by members. He believed that union procedures and rules should be respected by all and he was critical of unofficial activity. Some unofficial activity was promoted by a group called the Building Workers Charter who felt that rank and file members had too little say in the union. On one occasion a number of their supporters instigated a sit in at the head office of UCATT. After a few days, the sit in was ended. George maintained his view that the union's rules and procedures, if used properly, allowed for full democratic participation. Although he was at odds with those who took part in unofficial activities thereby undermining his official leadership, he bore them no malice. A leading light in unofficial activities in London was a former ASW shop steward called Jack Henry, a fierce critic and opponent of George's leadership. As a result of his activities in the Barbican strike in 1967, he had been blacklisted by employers and made jobless. Although George thought that Henry had discredited himself and the union by his very disruptive behaviour as a shop steward, years earlier, he recognised his unwarranted distress. He personally intervened with a building firm in London to get him a job and Henry, by his subsequent conduct, proved his worth to his employer as well as to his union.

Not long after UCATT had got its first breath, it was faced by a major test of its strength. Together with the other unions, it had submitted a claim for a substantial improvement in wages and hours in the building industry but the claim was resisted by employers. There was a strong feeling in UCATT that wages had fallen behind other industries. As a result, in 1972, strike action was called selectively and gradually extended so that it was eventually a country-wide strike and lasted thirteen weeks. Whilst the strike commanded the support of members of the trade unions in the industry there was no certainty about its outcome. As the general secretary of the principal union, George was acutely aware that it seriously threatened the union in its infancy and there was no certainty that it would survive into adulthood. UCATT's finances and the organisation of support were seriously challenged. Whilst four trade unions were party to the strike, George as the leading union official carried much of the responsibility on his shoulders.

In 1972, the strike in the building industry was on a scale without a parallel in the history of the industry. Enthusiastic rank and file activity, including support from unofficial groups, was an important ingredient on the union side. Eventually, the employers reluctantly conceded a package deal which the unions were willing to accept.

The strike was successful and achieved the largest ever increase in wages for building workers. Some UCATT members opposed the agreed terms ending the dispute and wished to pursue the claim for a reduction in hours. However, theirs was a minority view and did not prevail. In private, George would parody critics of the strike settlement by referring to himself as 'sell-out Smith'. The outcome of the strike was remarkable for only about one third of workers in the building industry were trade unionists. As a result of the success of the strike, George's leadership was recognised by his executive council and thereafter he exercised great personal authority over them. For George, the strike's success in raising basic pay nationally upheld his belief in the value of national settlements rather than settlements at lower levels. In the years immediately prior to the dispute he had thought that settlements nationally in the building industry had been eroded by bargaining at lower levels. The outcome of the strike established a good uniform standard of pay for all workers in the industry which was a goal that George always wanted to achieve.

Concomitant with the long period of negotiations and the strike itself, George served as president of the TUC when membership was ten million. As a result of the annual rotation of the office and his seniority he was elected by the general council for the period 1971 to 1972. The president chaired the monthly meetings of the general council and meetings of the general purposes committee and was consulted by the TUC general secretary on all major issues. The year of George's presidency was fraught. The Conservative government had introduced the 1971 Industrial Relations Act which imposed new restrictions on trade unions and as a result, the TUC was at loggerheads with it. During the year, George led many delegations from the TUC to meetings with the government. Throughout this period, there were a number of events during the year at which the trade union movement demonstrated its opposition to the new legislation. The Act challenged unions individually over how they would respond to the restrictions imposed by the legislation. It was characteristic of George that in deciding how best his own union should respond to the new legislative framework, he consulted academics in industrial relations at Oxford University. He was not content merely to rely on his experience alone but wanted to use theoretical expertise also. An additional worry for him during his presidential year was Doris's health. Doris was diagnosed with breast cancer for which an operation was necessary and she was in hospital for several days.

At the end of his year as president, George addressed the annual congress in September 1972. His address was intended to promote reflection amongst delegates rather than self-congratulation. He said that in the past year, the general council had defended the trade union movement against the attacks of the government's industrial relations act. However, he cautioned delegates that whilst trade unions must promote their case to the public they were not an alternative government. He advocated greater centralisation of trade unions for them to cope better with a world of multi-national companies. He suggested that rationalisation of trade unions structures and a review of procedures was also necessary. He observed that technological development imposed social change that people were powerlessness to control and led to social disenchantment. He said that although half the working population were not trade unionists the trade union movement had a responsibility for securing rights for all people. He proposed that trade unions be self-critical so that they were not narrowly focussed on their own sectional interests but could realise the aspirations of a greater proportion of workpeople than they were doing currently. The delegate who moved the vote of thanks for the presidential address said it was controversial in part but that was expected of George anyway.

Prior to his presidential year, George's responsibilities at the TUC had already increased by the creation of a construction committee in 1970, of which he was elected chair. It provided him and the other members with a platform to lobby for changes to improve the working lives of employees in the industry. The committee campaigned for measures to end the lump and also to decasualise employment. George also continued his membership of the economic committee and the commonwealth advisory committee. The most important committee of which he became a member was the Liaison Committee of the TUC and Labour Party. It was formed in 1970 to combat the industrial relations bill of the Conservative government. After the bill had become law, the Liaison Committee continued as a permanent body and George was appointed as one of the six representatives from the TUC. The purpose of the Liaison Committee in its new phase was to formulate the wider economic and industrial policies of the next Labour Government. It met monthly, both whilst Labour was in opposition and in office. For the members from the TUC, it afforded them unique access to the Prime Minister and senior ministers. George became more closely acquainted with Harold Wilson and subsequently James Callaghan, together with other Labour parliamentarians. During its life, the Liaison Committee provided the TUC with exceptional consultative status that distinguished it from all other pressure groups. George was a regular participant in these monthly meetings. According to another participant, Barbara Castle, he was prone to make earthy comments at the meetings.

Whilst George strongly supported Labour in government he was by no means uncritical of it. He expressed his opposition to government proposals for devolution in Scotland, in 1976, at the annual congresses of the Scottish TUC and TUC. He attacked the fallacious arguments of the nationalists who he accused of being enemies of the working class. He maintained that Scotland had sufficient autonomy and that devolution risked breaking-up the United Kingdom. He expressed his belief that an independent Scotland would not be economically self-sufficient. Instead of devolution, he argued for tough action by central government to even out inequalities in Britain and called for a united socialist Britain. The TUC and STUC rejected the motions that he moved.

At the 1976 annual congress of the TUC he also criticised the Labour government for its inaction over the Shrewsbury pickets who had been jailed for their part in the 1972 building strike. He demanded a parliamentary inquiry into the process by which the law had been used to secure their convictions. In 1977 he voiced criticisms of cuts in public expenditure that fell upon construction not only for their adverse effects on building workers but also because of their wider adverse impact.

Although George exerted a political influence as general secretary of UCATT, his political perspective baffled those he encountered, for they gave him labels that were contradictory. To those who engaged in unofficial union action, he was right wing. To Barbara Castle he was a moderate. She used the description, right wing, for parliamentary Labour colleagues for whom she felt contempt. To the Labour editor of the *Financial Times*, George was a left-winger. Perhaps the industrial relations journalist, Stephen Milligan, was the most accurate. In his threefold political categorisation of trade union leaders, he assigned George to the unpredictable category rather than to the left-wing or right-wing categories.

As UCATT general secretary, George's responsibilities increased beyond his own union and the TUC. The Advisory, Conciliation and Arbitration Service was established in 1974 and George was appointed to the Council that governed it. The purpose of ACAS was to provide information, advice, training, conciliation and other services for employers and employees to help prevent or resolve workplace problems. George was happy to accept the appointment for he strongly supported the purpose of ACAS.

For several weeks in 1975, Doris and George noticed that strange noises could be heard in the earpiece of the telephone at home when they picked it up for use. Doris suspected that the telephone was tapped and was most perturbed about this invasion of privacy.

George was more resigned in his response to the incidents. More two decades earlier he had been informed by an ASW official whose son was in the Glasgow Police that there was a special branch file on him. Since then, he had accepted that security records were probably kept on him because of his erstwhile membership of the Communist party and the senior offices that he held in the trade union movement. He accepted that trade union officials and Communist party members, past and present, were amongst the large category of individuals kept under surveillance because of suspected subversion. Of the records later released by the security services on individuals kept under surveillance, none was on George. However, not all security records have been released. In the same year as the suspected telephone tapping, George was given surgery for lung cancer. His admission to hospital necessitated sick leave for several weeks.

As a trade union leader, George accompanied by Doris, moved in social groups that were totally different from the social groups from which they sprang. They became used to meeting people, whose social origins were unlike their own, at social events to which they were invited. One such occasion was the dinner that they attended for the Shah of Persia in Downing Street in 1976. They enjoyed this event as they did many others where there were people from diverse social backgrounds but it was the company of blue collar union officials and their wives that they enjoyed best of all. The company of Scots was also much to the liking of George. For these were the people with whom he and Doris had much in common and who they liked.

George had long upheld the view that it was in the interests of trade unionists to cooperate fully with a Labour government to keep it in office. He therefore supported the Social Contract negotiated between the TUC and the Labour Party before the latter took office in 1974. The Social Contract implied that in return for moderating wage claims the unions could expect the government to increase the value of the social wage through means such as food subsidies, rent controls, tax concessions and higher pensions. However, by 1975 there was rampant inflation, leading many trade unionists to reject the restraints that they had initially accepted.

At the UCATT conference in 1976, there was a heated debate on the pay restraint that was integral to the Social Contract. George defended it but conference rejected his argument and voted in support of free collective bargaining. He was aghast at the conference decision and asserted that it was a breach of the trust between the union and the wider Labour movement. George's view was that if the Social Contract was not upheld, the country's economic problems would be aggravated. He believed that unless UCATT's rejection of the Social Contract was reversed, the Labour government would be imperilled. Further, he envisaged that the general public would not acquiesce to the authority of an elected government being usurped by the trade unions. If it were, he anticipated the replacement of the Labour government by a Conservative government before long. He firmly believed that such a turn of events would be to the detriment of the trade union movement. Therefore, he resolved to do what he could to bolster the Labour government by instigating a ballot of members to review the conference decision. The ballot was a risk for him personally because if it upheld the conference decision, his standing in his final years in office would be diminished. As it happened, the result of the ballot was for a reversal of the conference decision. George continued to support the pay restraint of the Labour government even after a tightening of the criteria for pay rises in summer 1978. By this time he was terminally ill on sick leave and therefore unable to translate his personal support for the government's policy, to union support. It was a source of frustration for him.

Before his retirement was due in 1979, George began to anticipate the event. He was nostalgic for Scotland and with Doris's agreement he began to make plans for a home in Arbroath to replace their home in Croydon. He envisaged a return to the place of his childhood with great pleasure. In contemplating the future, he was reconciled to prospect of a Scottish Parliament being established by the Labour government. In that event, he foresaw that he might satisfy his political aspirations in retirement through securing adoption as a Labour candidate for the new Scottish Parliament after he had retired to Arbroath.

In January 1978, George was awarded a knighthood in the New Year's honours list. Initially, when he was approached about the honour he declined. He felt that acceptance of a titled honour might suggest that he had abandoned his belief in social equality. After mulling over the matter and knowing that Doris felt that the honour was well deserved, he changed his mind and accepted it, having satisfied himself that his acceptance did not betray a cherished principle. In March 1978, the staff at the headquarters office of UCATT made a presentation to George to mark his award of a knighthood. They wanted to show that they shared the respect for him that his honour signified. Later in the year, when his terminal illness caused his absence from the UCATT conference, delegates showed their feelings by gifting a china dinner set to him and Doris.

Sir George Smith died on November 21, 1978 aged sixty four. His obituary in *The Times* newspaper described him as an influential union leader, a man of great shrewdness and integrity and a doughty bargainer. In its obituary to him, UCATT said that his forthright approach would be long remembered and it credited him with the merger of unions that formed UCATT and with having left behind a strong and powerful union. The membership of UCATT had increased from two hundred and sixty two thousand, two hundred and ten in 1971, to three hundred and thirty four thousand and ninety nine in 1978.

After George's death, Doris cancelled the plans made for a home in Arbroath because she did not wish to return to Scotland alone. Instead, she moved to Romiley, Stockport, to live near her daughter. At the invitation of UCATT, she attended its conference in 1980. The chairman told the conference that George was a special type of trade unionist and he was missed. He described him as a man of character; outspoken and compassionate and a man who had no rancour. James Callaghan, now Leader of the Opposition, addressed the conference. He said he was saddened that George had passed away because as Prime Minister he had received advice and assistance from him which he valued. He expressed his thanks to Doris, for what George 'had done for us all'.

Lady Doris Smith died on 2 July 1982, aged sixty seven.

George's legacy to UCATT did not endure for long, after his death. It was undermined by an inhospitable political environment and internal strife about the future of the union. In 2016, UCATT, much diminished in membership and resources, acceded to absorption by UNITE, the largest British trade union. By doing so, UCATT followed the prior example of other trade unions which had decided to secure their future through unity with a more powerful body.

Chapter 3

Uncovering the Roots of George and Doris

George and Doris brought eight family lines together. I made a substantial personal journey into my family history by tracking these lines as far back as possible. My knowledge of these eight lines at the start was very little indeed so all the lines emerged as great novelties. The more memorable experiences of my journey are described in this chapter.

With George, I started with his paternal line. It was my grandfather who prompted my first visit to an archive and it proved to be an impressive experience. I travelled to Angus Archives to inspect records that might illuminate family anecdotes of my paternal grandfather, James Guthrie Smith an active trade unionist and socialist in in Arbroath in the early 1900s. I really did not know what to expect and was delighted when I came across his name, several times in both the minutes of the Arbroath branch of the Independent Labour Party and the Arbroath branch of the National Union of Boot and Shoe Operatives. They confirmed that he was an active participant, holding office in both organisations. It was also fascinating to read about the political issues that engaged my grandfather's generation. World War One and the Russian Revolution were principal amongst them. To my great surprise, I found my grandfather listed as secretary of the Arbroath Proletarian or Socialist Sunday School which sought to promote socialist and secular values and beliefs. The records showed that he was totally committed to the pursuit of social justice and a more equal society. As a result of my research at Angus Archives, I was in no doubt that George had been influenced greatly in his upbringing by his father's political outlook. George had learned much about socialist ideas and the value of trade unions from his earliest age and he developed these ideas later in his life.

My continuing curiosity about George's paternal line took me to the National Records of Scotland in Edinburgh. I knew from church and statutory records that my 3x and 4x great-grandfathers, both called George Smith, had been agricultural labourers in Arbirlot, a parish adjacent to Arbroath. I knew that kirk session records could be illuminating about the lives of local people, whoever they were, and I wondered if my forebears might appear in them. Initially, I was disappointed, because the kirk session minutes for the period of interest had not survived. My disappointment was replaced by excitement when I found that the kirk accounts for this period had survived and my 4x great grandfather was listed in them several times from 1795. I found him with others who were in receipt of parish assistance in cash and kind. With the help of historical sources, I gained a fuller appreciation of his life. His low paid work was irregular and left him poor enough to qualify for assistance that was very basic in the standard it allowed. Yet, compared to the treatment of the poor throughout Scotland, he was treated well. I felt a mixture of sorrow and gratitude.

At the National Records of Scotland, I found that my 3x great-grandfather had been listed as liable for militia service during the Napoleonic war. Had he actually been conscripted, I wondered? A visit to The National Archives at Kew was necessitated. It showed that after five years of compulsory service, he had continued as a volunteer for a time which surprised me. His service as a volunteer suggested patriotism but my scrutiny of historical sources offered a more plausible explanation. For the unskilled and poor, being a part-time militiaman offered a means to stay above the breadline as well as an opportunity for patriotism. I felt I had gained an insight into the life of my forebear and the very hard times that faced him and his peers.

When I turned my attention to a second line descending to George, I encountered a surprise in the church and statutory records. I came across forebears who originated in the Highlands. In family anecdotes, there was never any mention of an ancestral connection with the Highlands. So I was fascinated to discover that I had forebears who were Gaelic speaking clans' people. The Highland line that descended to George had originated in Inverness-shire. These forebears migrated to Angus in the 1800s because the opportunities for farm work in the county were much greater than in the struggling Highlands. I was unable to trace this line before the late 1700s, which was disappointing. In this line, I was shocked by the circumstances surrounding the premature death of my 2x great-grandfather, Alexander Mclean, a railway labourer.

In researching a third line that descended to George, I was fascinated to discover forebears, who as common people, showed political consciousness, in a pioneering fashion, in the 1700s. The Fenwick forebears had had broken with the established church because of its domination by the landowners. With others, they formed a dissenting church. I was intrigued that one of these forebears, my 3x great-grandfather, Gilbert, had joined the army during the French revolutionary war. He became even more interesting when I found that he was a private in the battalion of a regiment that had mutinied over military discipline. This line of forebears were handloom weavers, and as such, in the forefront of those demanding democratic political reform in an undemocratic age. I felt that the dissenting outlook of these forebears had trickled down to George through his mother. I concluded that George's political outlook owed as much to his mother as to his father.

In uncovering a fourth line that descended to George, I found female forebears whose lives were very typical of the common people in that needlework was a principal domestic activity. However, one of the male partners of these female forebears stood out because of his achievement. He was my 3x great-grandfather, Thomas Murie, a shoemaker, who, during the Napoleonic war, joined the Royal Perthshire militia as a part-time private and made a career out of it. His service became full time as a non-commissioned officer and culminated in his appointment as a sergeant major. Perth & Kinross archives, I discovered, held a small collection on him including a diary that he kept in his early years. I felt that he was a forebear of humble origins, who had distinguished himself in his chosen path. I also felt there was a parallel between his life and George's. However, his lack of wealth had stopped him becoming a commissioned officer.

My tracking of George's four lines pulled his family history geographically from Angus and Dundee at the start of my research, to Perthshire, Fife and Inverness-shire at the finish.

When I began to research Doris's lines, I knew that her forebears had inhabited the disparate areas of Dundee and Orkney. I wondered if my findings would extend their geographical boundaries.

With her Ferguson line, I was able to establish that their connection with Dundee started soon after 1700 when a forebear had migrated from Angus. In Dundee, these forebears were at the heart of the city's economy – textiles and the harbour, in essence. It became very clear to me that this line was Dundee through and through. However, a mystery remained. Family anecdote said that my great-grandfather, David Ferguson, a mechanic, had visited India late in the 1800s. I made exhaustive searches of varied sources but failed to find evidence that corroborated the anecdote. On a hunch, I arranged to visit a cousin in Dundee, who might be able to help. From the annotated documentation that she showed me, I learned that my great-grandfather, David Ferguson, was employed in jute manufacture in Calcutta in 1882 and my 2x great-grandfather, also named David Ferguson had preceded him there for the same purpose in 1855. One mystery in my family history had been cleared up!

In Doris's forebears, I had long understood that one, my great-grandmother, Margaret Brown, was Stornoway-born. This fragment of information fascinated me because it suggested that she was of Hebridean ancestry. Could this suggestion be confirmed? My genealogical research confirmed that Margaret Brown had indeed been born in Stornoway in 1852 but she was not of Hebridean ancestry. Her parents were only temporary residents in Stornoway whilst her father was employed on the construction of a lighthouse. They were natives of Angus. Further research showed that Margaret Brown's maternal forebears had inhabited, for hundreds of years, Broughty Ferry, a fishing village on the outskirts of Dundee. So, Doris had lived within a few miles of her historic family village until she moved to Manchester in 1949. She never knew of her long family connection with Broughty Ferry. I felt that I had uncovered a remarkable degree of stability amongst this line of forebears.

Amongst my Broughty Ferry forebears, one individual emerged who particularly captured my interest, my 3x great-grandfather, Thomas Webster. I learned that he had started working life with his father as a fisherman, had joined the Royal Navy during the Napoleonic war and later transferred to the Coastguard in its years as an anti-smuggling force. Most remarkable of all, my inspection of records at The National Archives showed that at the age of thirteen, he had served in the Sea Fencibles - a naval militia of which I knew nothing until then.

In addressing the two Orcadian lines of descent to Doris, my initial understanding was that both lines inhabited the island of Sanday. Early on in my research, I found that only one line had inhabited Sanday, for the other line had inhabited the island of Westray. I wondered how far back in history had these forebears lived in Orkney and what way of life did they have? I visited

Orkney in 1973 and 1989 for holidays but I only began to get answers to my questions from burrowing into both records and historical sources. My research took me back to the early 1700s before these forebears disappeared from the church records or the church records themselves disappeared. The evidence I gathered suggested that both lines were long-time residents. The way of life of these forebears emerged from their lives as peasants/smallholders who also fished. It was fascinating to learn of the distinctive customs of these Orcadians. They shared their dwelling with their animals, the whole community occasionally supported a whale hunt and the seaweed, kelp, had several economic uses which made it important in their lives. I became very aware that their way of life was very different from my own!

With such a very stable history of settlement in the islands, I was left with one important question unanswered. Why in 1898 had my great-grandparents, Charles Drever and Ann Scott Peace, pulled up their roots to re-settle in a city on the eastern seaboard of Scotland? I gained an answer to my question from the historical sources I consulted. I learned that in the later 1800s, many Orcadians had left the islands to escape the very poor economic prospects from staying there. Those migrating to mainland Scotland used the available sea routes which were to the east coast. It dawned on me that I had missed the obvious! Nonetheless, I remained curious about the consequences of the migration. Had my great-grandparents made a better life for themselves? On a visit to Dundee City Archives, I collected information about, the Dundee Harbour Board, (Charles Drever's employer) and from other sources also. I concluded that my great-grandparents had significantly improved their standard of living from migrating to Dundee. I was aware, nonetheless, that I was unable to assess the losses that they had felt from their migration.

In my research into Doris's Orcadian lines, I explored the military service of my grandfather, Thomas Sinclair Maxwell Drever, in WW1. I knew only that he had been in the Royal Artillery, nothing more. His reticence about his experience was intriguing. With his service record and help from the Royal Artillery Museum, I was able to examine at The National Archives, the war diary for his time as a gunner. Although his time on the Western Front was relatively short, the danger to which he was exposed became clear and explained his reluctance to recall a fearful time. I was pleased to have cleared up another enduring puzzle.

Chapter 4

Almost Red Lichties

Arbroath is a small town at the mouth of the river Tay with a history that started with the foundation of Arbroath Abbey in 1178. Arbroath was a fishing port and a market town that served its immediate rural area in Angus, formerly known as Forfarshire. The term red lichtie is the local nickname for someone who comes from Arbroath. Originally, the red lichtie or red light was the flame which burned from the "Round O" of the ruins of Arbroath Abbey and was used to guide fishing boats back from the North Sea to the harbour. This chapter describes the paternal forebears of James Guthrie Smith as almost red lichties because they lived in parishes in Arbroath's agricultural hinterland. Moreover, Arbroath was important to their lives as the nearest market town, site of a hiring fair and centre of industrial growth and employment.

The surname Smith is the most common surname in Scotland as it is in the English –speaking world at large and the origins of the name are occupational. The name Smith comes from the Anglo-Saxon word smitan which means to smite or hammer. It was a generic term to describe anyone who hammered or struck objects whether wood, metal or stone. In the middle ages the metal worker was one of the earliest occupations requiring training and skill. He was important in village life for his expertise in making horseshoes, ploughshares, weaponry, armour and other items. The name has an uneven distribution in Scotland, with Angus as one of the three counties where its frequency is greatest.

The paternal family history of James Guthrie Smith, for which records have survived, starts with George, senior, an agricultural labourer who lived in Arbirlot and was reliant on poor relief intermittently. He was succeeded by his Arbirlot-born son George, also an agricultural labourer, who served in the militia for several years during the Napoleonic wars. The next direct forebear's life that is described is Inverkeillor-born John, senior, who started life as an agricultural labourer and ended it as a small farmer in Craig. The successor to John, senior, was Arbirlot-born John whose working life started as a ploughman and ended as a bleacher in Arbroath.

George Smith Senior

The earliest direct paternal forebear of James Guthrie Smith was George Smith, who lived in the parish of Arbirlot, from his marriage to Ann Gorty in 1781 until his death in 1817. He and Ann were to have eight children between 1782 and 1797. Ann Gorty was born in the parish of Glamis, Angus in 1753. Glamis was about seventeen miles from Arbirlot. If George was not born in Arbirlot, it was probably in another Angus parish close to Arbirlot. Ann was aged twenty eight on her marriage. The average age of marriage at this time was late twenties which suggests that George was aged about twenty nine at the time of his marriage and therefore born about 1752. His birth was after the Jacobite rebellion of 1745-1746. Many people of all classes in Angus, gentry included, were sympathetic to the cause of the rebels who dominated the county for a few weeks and occupied Arbroath. In the aftermath of the uprising, punishment was meted out to rebels and the county was unsettled for a period

George's early life was in a society where agriculture had changed little for hundreds of years. However, during his later life an agrarian revolution took place with huge social and economic consequences. At the time of George's birth, the bulk of the population of Scotland made their living by cultivating the land. The population remained largely peasant in character as it had been for hundreds of years. Only a tiny minority owned land which conferred great power on them. At the end of the 1700s, of Scotland's population of one million six hundred thousand, only seven thousand were landowners. Amongst the peasantry, there were divisions arising from the type of tenancy with the largest segment being cottars (also known as cottagers) who constituted up to half of the inhabitants in most places. Cottars were not always distinguishable from sub-tenants although the latter had stronger land rights. The cottars were highly prevalent in the population of the early 1700s and it was from this stratum that the landless agricultural labourers emerged, one of whom was George.

Cottars possessed small patches of land in return for the seasonal labour that they offered to larger holdings. They provided labour services for a number of days in the year. They held the merest fragments of land and so had to seek work in larger holdings to obtain full subsistence. The land they possessed was in strips and small plots and they engaged in communal practices (house building for example) in order to pool labour. Cottars lived in small settlements (fermtouns) of fifteen to twenty households that could be dispersed across the countryside rather than concentrated. They had grazing rights to some land and also made use of some common land. There was great stability for cottars tended to live and work in the same place all their lives. The agricultural system that prevailed before 1760 in Scotland ushered the male and female children of cottars into a period of landless farm service whilst in their teens and twenties. They became farm servants on the bigger farms where they lived with the farmer's family and were employed on contracts for periods of six months at a time. Reward was partly in money and partly in kind. At marriage they usually obtained a cottar holding. It is probable that George and Ann followed this path until their marriage. However, by this time the major transformation in agriculture was well underway and was removing the cottars. This transformation occurred in the period between 1760 and 1830. A consequence of that revolution occurring was that new methods were introduced into farming by landowners to improve agricultural production. The old system whereby cottars received small patches of land in return for service at important times of the year was replaced. Landowners forced tenants, sub-tenants and cottars off the land by increasing rents and serving eviction notices.

The removal of cottars from land in their possession in Arbirlot is confirmed by the *Old Statistical Account*. Fields were enclosed; common land taken over, strips of land were consolidated and the average size of farms increased. Gradual and piecemeal consolidation of tenancies displaced population and amounted to clearances in the Lowlands. These occurred earlier than those in the Highlands. The latter have remained in the public memory because they were conducted with greater brutality and at a time of greater social conscience. Crops and rotations were changed and ancient traditions of husbandry were destroyed. The whole framework of life of a largely agrarian population was transformed. The peasant economy where most people were engaged in production for themselves gave way to a society of capitalist farmers and landless labourers producing food for town and country. Single tenancies became common and multiple tenancies were reduced. As a result, the huge cottar population was removed. Some cottars left the countryside for the towns, a few became the new tenant farmers and many became landless agricultural labourers who were paid in money and kind. As agricultural labourers, they were still given scraps of land or gardens but were much less independent than before. The agricultural revolution in Scotland led to the end of a system of land management which had prevailed for hundreds of years and changed the life of the common people.

Arbirlot in George's lifetime was an agricultural parish of one thousand and fifty five people who lived in two hundred houses. The principal crops grown in the parish were oats, barley, wheat and turnips. They were grown in fruitful soil that was enriched by seaweed from the parish coastline and imported lime. In 1797, there were thirty eight tenant farmers who owned between them forty to fifty ploughs and one hundred and thirty eight farm horses. The farmer owning the largest number of farm horses, twelve, was an employer of George senior for a time. There was some cattle breeding and linen making was a cottage industry from the flax was that was grown, dressed, spun and weaved. Two mills helped with the early processing of the flax. George had several successive farm addresses implying that he was employed by different tenant farmers in Arbirlot.

There were four alehouses, one parish school and three mills engaged in grinding corn. From the river Elliot which ran through the parish, trout and salmon were caught. The parish was wholly in the ownership of the Maule family, specifically, the Hon. William Maule at this time, to whom rent was paid by all tenants. It also seems the parish possessed a healthy air and there were no peculiar diseases.

George, as an agricultural labourer was exposed to the economic risks of that occupation. Work was not always available on a regular basis and even when it was, the remuneration was meagre. Consequently he received outdoor poor relief for his household on an intermittent basis over the years, especially later in his life.

On April 5 1795, he was paid one allowance of 5s from the parish poor's fund. He was next paid in 1807, several allowances which totalled £1 3s 6d for the year. In 1808 he received five allowances totalling £3 14s 0d for the year. In 1809 he was paid seven allowances and the sum totalled £4 5s 10d. In 1810 he was paid allowances which totalled £1 12s 0d. He received no allowances in 1811. In 1812, on 15 June he was paid 10s which was his only allowance during that year. In 1813 he received five allowances totalling £1 5s 0d. In 1814 he was paid only one allowance of 6s. He was not listed a recipient of the poor's fund after 1814. The significance of these allowances is shown by the usual pay for farmworkers in Arbirlot in 1791. The yearly pay of male farm servants was £7 to £8 and for day labourers (who provided their own food) the pay was 12d to 15d per day.

George was also a recipient, between 1809 and 1814, of the free oatmeal that was distributed to the poor of the parish. The oatmeal was distributed either in late December or early January each year. In 1809 and 1814 George received one boll, and for each year in between, three firlots. The records for distribution of the oatmeal for 1814 to 1822 have not survived. The oatmeal was distributed using the old Scots dry measures of bolls, firlots and pecks. A boll was constituted by four firlots and a firlot was constituted by sixteen pecks. One boll weighed about one hundred and forty pounds and a peck was about eight and a half pounds.

The assistance in cash and kind given to George was legitimated by the Old Poor Law. Under this system, which lasted in Scotland between 1574 and 1845, the parish authorities, the kirk session (church court) and the heritors (landowners) were jointly responsible for relieving the poor. In Arbirlot, they exercised this responsibility principally by paying cash allowances at monthly intervals and distributing free oatmeal annually. The number of recipients of poor relief in the parish each year between 1795 and 1814 was between twenty and thirty.

The kirk session (comprising the minister and the elders of the kirk and numbering about twelve usually) was responsible for moral discipline in the parish and administered assistance to the poor. The parish operated a fund for the poor and the income was raised from church collections, fines on offenders and fees for carrying out sacraments and services, like the use of mortcloths at funerals. Although in some parishes, (a minority), funds for the poor were raised from a tax levied on the owners of land or property, Arbirlot chose to rely on voluntary contributions to the poor's fund. The kirk session in Arbirlot, as in all the other parishes, exercised discretion in fulfilling its obligations to the poor of the parish. It determined the criteria for granting relief and the amount of allowance. There was no fixed national standard to follow.

It is not apparent how much the sole heritor in Arbirlot contributed to the poor's fund but his reputation suggests that he was a generous contributor. The heritor was the Hon. William Maule who became the landowner of the parish in 1787 until his death in 1852. He owned much land in Angus and was one of the richest men in Scotland. He was elected as a Whig MP in 1796, held high office in the freemasons and in 1831 was raised to the peerage as Baron Panmure of Brechin & Navar. After his death he was described as an excellent landlord, highly popular among his many tenants and the labourers on his estates, whom he treated with great liberality. In 1839 his tenants erected a statue, one hundred and five feet high, as a memorial of their respect for him as their landlord. He was credited with unceasing acts of benevolence. One of these acts was an annuity of fifty pounds to the widow of Robert Burns, which was continued until the eldest son of the poet was able to provide for his mother.

In addition to its poor's fund, Arbirlot had a mortification or legacy for the poor. Not all parishes had one. It meant that the financial assistance given to the poor was supplemented by the Mortified Meal Crop which was a bequest of a former landowner of the parish, Alexander Irvine. In 1622 there was a poor harvest and famine occurred throughout the country. In 1629 the Mortified Meal Crop was started in the parish when Irvine bound himself and his heirs to pay annually, twelve bolls of oatmeal to the poor of the parish. The grant was confirmed in 1637 by his son, Sir Alexander

Irvine. When the ownership of Arbirlot changed hands in 1679, the Earl of Panmure of the day and his successors maintained the legacy. George benefitted from this mortification.

Oatmeal was gifted to the poor because it was an important part of the basic diet in Scotland. In the early 1700s, labouring people were often paid partly in oatmeal and even the relatively privileged consumed vast and regular quantities of oatmeal. For a labouring family's budget, expenditure on oatmeal could be the largest single item, comprising a third of the annual budget. Oatmeal was recognised as an energy giving fuel for the labouring population that was relatively cheap, being a crop that was widely grown throughout the country as it was suited to the climate.

The level of support given to recipients of poor relief in Arbirlot, was upheld by the successive parish ministers in 1791 and 1835 in their contributions to the *Old and New Statistical Accounts.*

In 1791 the minister, Richard Watson, who served the parish between 1790 and 1829 claimed that there were few who were poor in the parish and as a result they were tolerably well provided for. He further maintained that the kirk session was knowledgeable about the local community and was able to respond to the needs of the poor. The session was very concerned to ensure that they met appropriately the necessities of everyone in the parish. The kirk session discharged its responsibility to the poor well and none of them had to resort to begging. The only begging in the parish was by vagrants who the minister considered dissolute and idle. He wanted them to be sent to workhouses. Overall, he took the view that the people of the parish were liberal to the poor.

In 1835 the Minister, Thomas Guthrie, who served the parish between 1830 and 1837, shared the view of his predecessor in concluding that provision for the poor of the parish was adequate. He thought that there was no other way of providing money for the poor than by established methods. Moreover, he opined that no other way of raising money for the poor was necessary. He observed that money had been saved from the poor's fund in recent years and that the annual fund for the poor was £80 compared to £35 in 1791 when the population was larger. He also inferred that only those who were in serious need would apply for assistance and that it was always as a last resort on their part.

The judgement of the two successive Ministers in Arbirlot that the poor of the parish were well provided for is upheld to some extent by evidence about poor relief generally in Scotland. Compared to other parishes, the poor relief given to George in Arbirlot was generous. This is shown by a comparison of average yearly expenditure on recipients of poor relief in different synods. There were approximately nine hundred parishes in Scotland and they were organised into synods on a regional basis. An estimate for 1818 showed that Angus and Mearns synod (which included Arbirlot), spent £4 3s 3d. Of the fifteen synods in Scotland, Angus and Mearns was the fifth most generous. The proportion of the population unable to subsist without some help was very similar across Scotland but the willingness of the parishes to raise funds differed because some parishes sought to keep allowances as low as possible. This was illustrated by the yearly expenditure of only 16s 11d on recipients of poor relief by Ross synod. In many parts of the Highlands and far north, the most that adults could expect was five shillings a year in money and a licence to beg within the parish. George was treated more generously than that.

The relatively generous poor relief given to George seems attributable in part to him living in a rural area rather than an urban area. Support given in urban areas was harsher. Relief was restricted to those legally entitled to it. There were many factors responsible for this meanness. A more complicated and bureaucratic system developed in urban areas like Glasgow and Dundee. The able bodied (physically fit) poor, of which George was one, whether they were in or out of work, were rarely granted assistance from public funds in urban areas. The poor who were considered deserving were orphans, the aged and the severely disabled. The Old Poor Law did not officially provide for the able-bodied who were usually labelled as the undeserving poor. As such, they were considered to be responsible for the circumstances that beset them. Their moral failings or bad behaviour was held to be the cause of their poverty and therefore material assistance was not considered a solution to their problems. In the urban areas a low level of expenditure on poor relief was equated with high moral standards by administrators of the system.

In Arbirlot, George received poor relief that was administered by the minister and elders of the Kirk. In many parishes, elders of the kirk were respected men who were appointed for life and they became familiar with the needs of the local inhabitants. In rural parishes, they could be very liberal to legitimate applicants for poor relief. Therefore the relief given to George was probably decided by tenant farmers who had employed him over the years. In small communities such as Arbirlot, the inhabitants knew each other well from their frequent social contact. Consequently, George destitute circumstances were not attributed to his moral failings. Those deemed of bad character, were given little support or none at all for they were the undeserving poor. Instead his support continued on an irregular basis for several years. Clearly in the eyes of the Kirk, he was seen as a man of good character. He was accepted as in need rather than irresponsible. Accordingly, he was given the relatively generous support that Arbirlot, as a rural parish, provided to its poor.

Whilst George was apparently given generous support by Arbirlot parish in comparison with the help given by many other parishes, the assistance given to him was unlikely to have been adequate. For the Old Poor Law was based on the principle that poor relief for the able-bodied was a supplement to other forms of income. It was not intended to be sufficient to meet all the necessities of the day for there was an expectation that recipients would call upon other sources of funds such family, charity or be able to earn a little in some way. Therefore poor relief was not intended to ensure a subsistence standard of living for the physically fit, by itself. When the Old Poor Law was reviewed by a Royal Commission in 1844, thirty years after George was a recipient, it concluded that allowances were often inadequate both in town and country parishes and the amount of relief given was frequently altogether insufficient to provide for even the common necessaries of life. A rule from the start of the Old Poor Law was that applicants were not to rely on it alone to meet their needs for they must also secure resources from their own efforts. Self-reliance was a key principle of the Old Poor Law.

It has been estimated that between 1807 and 1816 the average number of people in receipt of relief each year was forty four thousand, one hundred and ninety nine or 2.5% of the total population in Scotland. This measure of poverty does not show those who did not apply for relief or those who were denied relief (many of whom were similar to George in being physically fit but destitute). So the poor relief statistics seriously underestimated the level of poverty in Scotland. Many more were poor than those officially recognised as such. It was only granted to a select few and only as a last resort. So it might be inferred that George Smith senior was one of a fortunate few. The unfortunate many often had to resort to begging.

The large number of people living in or on the margins of poverty during George's life included many of the agricultural population. Other than the landowners and better off tenant farmers, there were many sub-tenants, cottars and labourers, whether paid daily or weekly, whose economic existence was precarious. Remuneration for them, whether in kind or cash, was unpredictable and unreliable. Poor weather and bad harvests were just two of the factors that caused fluctuations in earnings. However, the basic pay was very meagre anyway. Married labourers at the end of the 1700s in the Lowlands had earnings considerably below what was required to feed, clothe and house their families, even when such a household had possession of a smallholding to grow vegetables. It seems that few agricultural labourers and their families escaped the need to call upon parish relief at some time during their lives. For labourers at the end of the 1700s and beginning of the 1800s, it was a time of struggle to make ends meet. The irregular nature of allowances paid to George indicates that his work and earnings fluctuated considerably. As a labourer, he was exposed to considerable hazards and lacked economic security. There was probably little or no difference in the standard of living of George's household living on, or off, poor relief.

The household income of agricultural labourers depended on the contributions made by their wives and children with or without poor relief. Spinning was a chief indoor occupation of females in Arbirlot in the 1700s and early 1800s and so Ann Gorty may have obtained earnings from spinning of linen. The children still living in the parental home when poor relief was given could have contributed their earnings from tasks such as hoeing, picking and sowing.

Agricultural labourers usually had access to a plot of ground for their own use upon which they grew vegetables and if it was large enough, raise livestock. The kale patch was always an important element of the agricultural labourer's household income in kind. Failing that, destitute agricultural labourers could appeal to past employers either for the use of a plot or for donations of food in return for undertaking small jobs.

In making ends meet, agricultural labourers and their families took advantage of what was free in the parish by foraging. Trout and salmon could be caught in the river Elliot, rabbit or other wildlife snared. Berries and other edible wild plants could be harvested. Poaching was a risky option although it was absent from the parish in 1835, according to the minister.

In his later years, one or more of George's eight children may have increasingly helped him to get by. After 1814 he received no poor relief. It seems improbable, given his advancing years as an agricultural labourer, that he and Ann no longer needed poor relief. In 1813, his address was Spinning Mill, Arbirlot which after 1815 became the address of his son George, on his return to Arbirlot from the adjacent parish of Carmyllie. It seems that family care was substituted for poor relief.

George died in Arbirlot in 1817 at the age of about sixty five. No record of the death of Ann Gorty has survived.

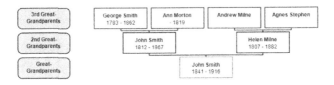

George Smith

George was born in 1783 in Arbirlot. Like his father, he was an agricultural labourer in Angus throughout his life. He was a militiaman for a time, and then in 1811 married Ann Morton, with whom he had four children. A widower in 1819, he later lived in the household of his son, John.

George was conscripted into the 1st Arbroath Battalion of the Forfarshire Militia in February 1801, several months before his eighteenth birthday in June. The Battalion was one of several that comprised the Forfarshire Militia. His prior notice of this event was probably seeing his name posted on the front door of the Arbirlot Kirk as one of sixty eight men in the parish, listed as eligible to serve. As a militiaman, he was a part-time soldier and one of approximately nine thousand in Scotland and forty thousand in England and Wales.

The regiment into which George was conscripted was one of the county infantry regiments raised in 1798 from conscripts and volunteers as auxiliary forces for internal defence because the regular army was stretched to the limit in home defence and foreign campaigns. This was the period of French revolutionary and Napoleonic wars which lasted between 1793 and 1815. The formation of the regiment was a result of the Militia Act Scotland, 1797. The purpose of the militia was to prepare for the defence of the country should there be an invasion by the French. A secondary purpose was to quell domestic disorder should it arise during the war with France.

To fulfil its responsibilities for home defence, the militia engaged in training and exercises. In peacetime, the militia were required to undertake a minimum of twenty four days of training annually. An important part of training was instructing recruits in the use firearms, usually firing a musket and wielding it with a fixed bayonet. The most intensive period of service in the militia for George was between February 1801 (when he started) and December 1801 which involved ninety one days duty. This lengthy period of duty was for basic training.

In 1805 George was stationed in Dundee Barracks on permanent duty for twenty one days. Some of the Battalion were despatched to Perth but the individuals concerned were not identified in the records. This activity by the Battalion suggests that one of the benefits of militia service for George was that it extended his experience by taking him to places that were completely unknown to him. Without that experience, he may never have left the district surrounding Arbirlot. Militia regiments were usually stationed as far away from their home districts as possible, to avoid any conflict between their military duties and their civilian loyalties.

George served five conscripted years in the militia and extended his service by at least two years as a volunteer. He was still a militiaman in September 1808 but records for the Arbroath Battalion after that date have not survived. Between February 1801 and September 1808 George's service in the Forfarshire Militia was three hundred and ten days for which he was paid a total of £15 and 5 shillings. Because of a gap in the records for the whole of 1803, his days of service for that year are omitted from the figure given above.

From his conscription as a part-time soldier, George received a bounty on enlistment and was paid a shilling a day for each day his battalion was periodically assembled. He was provided with a uniform and allowances for food and drink. He was a private in one of the three companies that constituted the Arbroath Battalion of the Forfarshire Militia. A company was constituted by a commanding officer who was usually a Captain, two Lieutenants, three Sergeants, two corporals, two drummers and sixty-six privates. The commanding officer of George's company was Captain William Hill and later William Colvill, who achieved promotion from Captain to Lieutenant Colonel. A property qualification was required for appointment as commissioned officer. Officers and other ranks were from different social classes and a definite social distance can be imagined between them. However, privates in the militia were agricultural labourers and other manual workers. Therefore leaving officers to one side, George's comrades in arms were men with whom he had much in common.

George's conscription into the militia suggests that he was healthy and poor. Had he been either disabled or persistently ill, he could have been exempted from conscription. In addition, his militia record showed no absence from sickness. His limited means meant that he could not buy his way out of conscription. Those who could pay a penalty of at least £10 could secure exemption or arrange (by financial inducement) for a substitute. A very high proportion of conscripted men indeed, were substitutes. Consequently, those conscripted were overwhelmingly from the poorer urban and rural classes, of which George was one.

Between 10% and 16% of conscripts deserted from the militia but George did not. Desertion was an expression of hostility to conscription in Scotland which many also opposed through rioting and civil disobedience. The opposition was principally to the infringement of liberty. George did not share this view for he volunteered to extend it by at least two years.

Much volunteering for military service between 1793 and 1815 was as a result of patriotic fervour instigated by the governing classes. Hundreds of thousands volunteered either for the voluntary regiments which had been formed, or for the militia. A more credible reason than patriotism for George volunteering was the additional income that a militiaman obtained. The militia's payments for occasional days of duty provided a guaranteed amount of income that supplemented his customary meagre and irregular earnings from being an agricultural labourer and helped to keep him above the breadline. Moreover, being a militiaman, fitted in well with his casual employment in agriculture, where a job could be easily left and picked up again later. Perhaps he recognised other personal benefits from being a militiaman such as a broadening of experience, particularly from travelling much further from home than would otherwise be possible Militia service could be a political education - on occasion militiamen were called upon to supress disturbances such as food riots although in some instances they refused to do so out of sympathy for the protesters. George may also have developed reading and writing skill and enjoyed the comradeship and solidarity of the militia.

Although, soldiering may have had advantages for George, it was not sufficiently appealing for him to follow the example of others and become a full-time soldier. The money may have been good as a full-time soldier but not good enough to compensate for the full-time military discipline imposed and the risks from combat with the enemy, France. In due course he decided to call time on his service in the militia, before his marriage to Ann Morton in 1811. After his discharge from the militia, his search for work took him to three parishes in the vicinity of Arbroath before he returned to home territory.

For agricultural labourers, continuity of employment was not common and it was necessary for other work to be undertaken to survive. George worked as a flax dresser in Inverkeillor parish and may have in Arbirlot too. According to the *Old Statistical Account*, flax raising, watering, dressing and spinning were important elements in the parochial economy of Arbirlot. There was one mill in Arbirlot engaged in cleaning flax and another engaged in dressing the same. Therefore, when George could not find work on the land, he probably worked as a flax dresser. Flax was the fibre used to make linen. It was a fairly demanding crop needing well-watered and fairly heavy soils. When the seeds were beginning to ripen, the crop was pulled up by the roots. Flax growing and its conversion into cloth had a very long history in Angus. Its importance grew importance in the 1700s and in the early 1800s Angus had more than half of the linen trade for Scotland as a whole. Flax growing was prevalent throughout much of the county. Flax growing and linen making had long been a domestic activity but it gradually became more industrialised. Arbroath, Montrose, Brechin and Kirriemuir became centres of the industry in Angus.

Flax dressing was a process whereby the flax was prepared for spinning by removing the straw. Firstly the flax was beaten until soft and then the flax was scraped to remove some of the straw. Finally the flax was pulled through combs to remove the last of the straw and also to polish the fibres. Flax fibres were turned into linen fabrics in large quantities. Fine flax was used for items such as lace. Course flax was used in the making of rope and twine. Linseed oil was a by-product of flax.

In being a flax dresser, George was in distinguished company for in 1777, the poet Robert Burns had tried it, on his father's farm for six months but abandoned it because it did not suit his health or inclination. Flax dressing was in part a repellent occupation. After harvesting and before dressing began, flax stems were tied up in stooks, and placed in water-filled pits for retting (meaning 'rotting'), decomposing through bacterial action for a week or two, producing the most awful stench, but softening the glue between the plant fibres.

George was followed in the occupation of flax dresser by at least one descendant who was an apprentice flax dresser in Arbroath in 1891.

Four children were born to George and Ann between 1812 and 1817 but their marriage was short-lived for she died in Arbirlot in March 1819, a month after the death of George's elder brother John.

Their deaths suggest an outbreak of infectious disease had occurred in Arbirlot. George was only thirty five when this tragic event made him a widower responsible for bringing up four children aged seven and under. In countenancing his catastrophic loss, George appears to have drawn on two sources of support. His younger unmarried sister Isabel moved in with him and took responsibility for the home and children and was still living under the same roof as him two decades later. The Kirk helped George to cope with widowerhood, and at the end of his life, he was still a communicant. During George's lifetime, many in the lower social strata defected from the Kirk to join seceding Presbyterian churches, most conspicuously after the Great Disruption of 1843. Prominent amongst the defectors were oppressed peasants and the upwardly mobile in urban areas. George did not defect and neither did his son John. Their loyalty to the Kirk suggests the influence of living in a traditional rural community where the local Kirk personified the community and the landowners accepted and fulfilled obligations to their social inferiors.

After the death of his wife, George continued to work as an agricultural labourer in Arbirlot. When his son John had formed his own household after his marriage, George joined it and in 1849 moved with it when John took possession of a small farm. George then worked for his son who could employ his father on lighter more menial jobs when heavy manual work outstripped his declining physical strength. George had retired from work before he died in 1862 at the age of seventy nine after a life of rude health.

John Smith Senior

John, the eldest son of George and Ann, was born in 1812 in Inverkeillor, near Arbroath, and in 1829 at the age of seventeen he married twenty two year-old Helen Milne. The average age of marriage was mid-twenties so John's early marriage may have been influenced by the straitened circumstances that followed the premature death of his mother. He had five sons and two daughters with Helen Milne between 1829 and 1852. Of these children, two died in childhood. He and Helen found work on the land in three parishes in the vicinity of Arbroath.

As the children of agricultural labourers, the working lives of John and Helen began at about the age of eight. From then on they began to learn to do jobs such as scaring birds, weeding or picking out stones from the fields, roads and tracks. Stones could blunt the blades of horse drawn ploughs and make roads uneven thereby causing damage to wagons and carts which used them so there was continued activity to remove them. Children progressed into the skilled aspects of work as they grew older. Later on in their lives, the children learned the full range of skills and activities of an agricultural labourer according to the seasonal calendar. The seasonal calendar meant that the agricultural labourer had a variety of work. It included sowing, ploughing, threshing, flailing, reaping, winnowing, harrowing, harvesting, liming and manuring fields, road, fence and drainage mending, hedging and coppicing, planting, hoeing, hay making, attendance on farm animals, carriage of various items and purchase of materials such as manure and seed.

Arbroath was the place where hiring fairs were held once or twice a year. At the hiring fairs farmers and individual workers struck bargains. The reputation and appearance of those seeking work counted as well as the conditions of work and food of particular farms. Remuneration was still largely in kind. The hiring fairs served a radius of twenty to thirty miles and therefore drew people from several adjacent parishes. Contracts for work usually lasted for six months for the unmarried or a year for the married but they could also be renewed and last for several years. Fortunately for John, the farmers of the Arbroath district had a preference for married farmworkers rather than unmarried so he did not need to travel far to obtain work and a family cottage. Nevertheless, because the accommodation of the agricultural labourer was often a cottage rented from his employer it changed every time he changed his employer. By the time of John was an adult, the cottages were usually a minimum of two rooms, sometimes with wooden flooring, plastered walls and ceilings, no ovens for home baking and with little furniture. They were stark and functional. The routine of work meant the labourer had to walk two or three miles to the main farm buildings (and home again) for the six working days of the week. Hours of work were eight to ten hours with a short break for lunch. It was common for the wives of labourers and their children to be busy working in the fields although compared to their adult male counterparts, the weeks they worked tended to be fewer and the hours in the day less.

Around 1848, John and Helen moved to the coastal parish of Craig to take possession of twelve acres of arable land. Agricultural labourers did progress to being farmers when, for example, they were lent money by a previous employer. The pay of an agricultural labourer was not usually sufficient to allow for any saving to set up a farm or smallholding. By this time John had a lengthy experience of farming which he had started at a young age. The attraction of a farm tenancy or small holding to an agricultural labourer was that it offered more independence and control over work as well as stability from a settled place of work and home. The farm was rented from William MacDonald MacDonald, a resident of Edinburgh whose land ownership in the district included a castle, its gardens and grounds, several farms, a reading room and female school house and a salmon fishery. The land was leased for less than nineteen years at an annual rent of £4. At twelve acres, the farm was small but by no means exceptional in size. Angus had an even distribution of small, medium and large farms. In 1875, the proportion of farms under twenty acres in the county was 41%. The farm was sometimes described as a croft as were four similarly sized neighbouring farms. This description of the farm coupled with its small size suggests that John may have been required to supply occasional help as a day labourer to larger tenant farmers or to the landowner.

To start with when the children were young, John employed a young farm servant to help him and Helen run the farm. Ten years later, there was no farm servant. The three children at home were now of an age to be able to help with the farm. John died in 1867 at the age of fifty four. The tenancy of the farm passed to his son, David and Helen continued to live there with David and his family, until her death, aged seventy five, in 1882. David kept the farm going for a few years until he relinquished it and returned to being an agricultural labourer in an adjacent parish.

John Smith

John, the son of John and Helen was born in 1841 in Arbirlot. John had a succession of jobs during his life: agricultural labourer, railway porter, quarryman and yarn bleacher. He married Ann Margaret McLean in 1864 and they had nine children in seventeen years. As a result of bereavement early in their marriage they extended their parental responsibility to Ann's two younger siblings and her nephew. They lived in parishes near Arbroath and latterly in the town itself.

When John moved to Craig parish at about the age of seven, there were four schools and there was no individual in the parish that was unable to read. Therefore, he probably benefitted from regular schooling simultaneously with providing some child labour. For the working life of the agricultural worker in the Scottish Lowlands began at eight or nine when the children were employed some of the time to do simpler tasks from which they contributed to the family budget. At about the age of thirteen of fourteen, they were in full-time farm service and performed miscellaneous tasks. In this phase they were classed as halflins. From about the age of seventeen, as a result of their prior preparation, most of the boys became ploughmen (or horsemen). By the time that John was employed, farm labour in the Lowlands had become specialised and hierarchical with the ploughman held in greatest esteem and paid accordingly. The ploughman was in sole charge of a pair of horses with a standard working day of ten hours. The horses were used to perform other tasks besides ploughing alone.

By the age of nineteen, John was employed as a ploughman in Bervie, Kincardineshire, on a farm that was three hundred and fifteen acres. Kincardineshire has since been absorbed by Aberdeenshire. The hiring fair had taken him sixteen miles north of his parents' farm in Craig. His home in Bervie, in 1861, was a bothy which he shared with two other young ploughmen, who were natives of Kincardineshire. Almost uniquely in Scotland, in Kincardineshire and much of Angus, unmarried farm hands were commonly housed by farmers in bothies. The farmers did not want their workers living with their family as in earlier periods of history. The bothy was a dormitory building where the farmworkers were expected to look to their own needs. Bothies could be simply sheds sheltering upto twenty four farm hands. Often there was no privy nor was the bothy subject to regular cleaning. It provided a very basic standard of accommodation and the inhabitants received an allocation of oatmeal, milk, potatoes and possibly coal. Remuneration was still largely in kind. The bothymen sold as much as half of their oatmeal and with the proceeds bought bread, tea, and syrup. With their long hours, the bothymen were socially isolated. Bothy life was harsh and demoralising.

Given the quality of life in a bothy, it is understandable that John did not stay in one for very long. In 1864 he had left Kincardineshire and agriculture to try his hand at a different type of manual labour, as a railway porter. John was now living in the village of Leysmill in Inverkeillor parish near Arbroath. Leysmill station was one of six intermediate stations on the railway line between Arbroath and Forfar that had opened in 1838. The line was opened primarily for the transport of freight, especially seaborne coal from Arbroath and quarry stone to Arbroath for further transportation by sea. However, by 1848 passenger traffic contributed 40% of gross revenue of this line. The main source of railway labour was from agriculture because the wages of farm workers were low so that the starting pay for porters secured applicants easily. The pay of a porter was several shillings a week better than an agricultural labourer. There were also some non-monetary additions such as free clothing. The physical standards were fairly high for porters as they were expected to be in good health with physical strength and good eyesight. The railway porters were the most numerous of all the railway employees and the least skilled. The drawback of the occupation was the seven day week and hours of duty that could amount to fifteen hours a day. There was also a strict disciplinary regime and a high rate of accidents and sickness in the industry.

In December 1864 twenty three year old John, married Ann Margaret Mclean, also aged twenty three and a domestic servant of highland descent. Their marriage was in the Free Church of Scotland, in Leysmill village. The Church was founded after the 'Great Disruption' of 1843 when over a third of Ministers and congregations broke away from the established Church of Scotland over the principle of patronage that was upheld by the State. The seceders believed that congregations should be able to exercise their choice in the appointment of Ministers without having to accept the veto of landowners, if the latter chose to use it. In supporting the Free Church, John and Ann Margaret behaved like many of their social peers who felt alienated by the Kirk.

In 1867, John and Ann Margaret were living in Johnshaven, Kincardineshire. His employer had posted him to the station there. The Montrose and Bervie railway was opened in 1865 and Johnshaven as one of the intermediate stations on this single track coastal branch line. In 1866, the Arbroath and Forfar railway and the Montrose and Bervie railway passed into the ownership of the Caledonian Railway company. It was customary for railway employees, particularly porters, to be moved for the building and extension of new lines.

There was a high voluntary turnover of Victorian railway employees (a length of employment of two and a half years was common) and by 1869 John had turned his back on the industry and returned to agriculture in the Arbroath area where he and Ann Margaret had formerly lived. In returning to agricultural labouring, he took a less well paid job than railway porter. However, his employment opportunities were limited by the skills that he could offer. The Arbroath area, unlike other parts of Angus, preferred married farm workers and made suitable accommodation available.

John and Ann now lived in St Vigeans, the parish that straddled urban Arbroath and its rural surroundings. In 1891 the civil parishes of Arbroath and St Vigeans were unified. John remained as an agricultural labourer for three or four years before eschewing it to become a quarryman for a few years. The pay on average for general labourers such as quarrymen was better than for agricultural labourers.

As a quarryman, John Smith was employed in an industry that stretched across Angus from east to west; there were several quarries in the district surrounding Arbroath. One was Letham quarry in St Vigeans parish and another was Leysmill quarry which was only two rail stops away from Arbroath. In becoming a quarryman, John Smith was continuing with outdoor work which he had been used to in his time as an agricultural worker.

The quarries near Arbroath were part of the geological formation of Angus known as Old Red Sandstone. This granite was solid in composition, very durable, and easily worked and dressed. It was extensively used, not only for paving streets, but for all inside work of houses, and for other purposes. The commercial name for the stone was 'Arbroath pavement' and it was of a high quality and reputation. It was used for many edifices, public and private in Scottish towns and cities and also exported abroad. Machinery was used extensively in the Angus quarrying industry to cut the stone away, shape it and prepare it for its intended uses. The quarries around Arbroath were important enough to prompt the manufacture of quarrying machinery in the town. The machinery in the quarries considerably reduced the scope for manual labour as in working with a sledge hammer. However, manual labour was still needed to transport the stone by loading it onto carts, steering the carts to the nearest railway station and unloading them.

In working in quarrying, John was exposed to the hazards of the industry. In general, quarries were dangerous places where blocks of stone were being lifted and transported daily and there was no safety equipment. Quarries were similar to mines with many accidents, of which a high number were fatalities. Quarrying was one of the most dangerous industries to work in with very little regulation to combat the intrinsic hazards.

By 1881, John had abandoned quarrying in favour of the textile industry. His work was now indoors and unlike his previous occupations, protected from severe weather that could halt work and result in a loss of pay. He had become a yarn bleacher in an industry in Arbroath that was at the height of its success.

The textile industry was boosted in Arbroath's economy in the late 1700s. The town had earlier been developing as a centre for handloom weaving, and this industry was augmented by steam-powered flax, textile and engineering works which were built along the Brothock Burn. By the late 1700s over one million yards of osnaburg cloth and brown linen were stamped as being produced in Arbroath. Sailcloth weaving alone supported five thousand jobs and attracted many workers from the surrounding rural parishes. By 1875 there were thirty four spinning mills and factories operating one thousand and four hundred power looms and producing four hundred and fifty thousand yards of cloth annually. In addition, bleach fields, tanneries, calendaring works, flourished. Although the industry was originally based on turning flax into cloth, it diversified during the 1800s and extended its range to other fibres, namely jute and tow (hemp).

Although the textile industry dominated Arbroath's economy when John became an employee, soon afterwards it began to decline as spectacularly as its earlier growth. The decline of the industry occurred for a variety of reasons including the increased use of cotton instead of linen and the shift from sail to steam vessels. However, John was employed by the industry until his very latest years.

As a yarn bleacher, John was employed by one of the bleachfields in Arbroath, of which there were seven in 1876 and four in 1915. The term bleachfield survived from the past before the introduction of chemical processes in a continuous factory system. In the past, bleaching was partially carried out by 'grassing' or laying the cloth out in the fields.

As a bleacher, John Smith worked in an industry in which machinery was used to put the textiles through several processes. Bleaching was a necessary preliminary to the dyeing of cloth. Bleaching involved the use of several chemicals such as sulphuric acid and processes which included steeping, boiling, scalding, washing and drying with various forms of machinery. Large cylindrical vessels called kiers were used in the bleaching process. The process of linen bleaching was a prolonged affair that involved repetition and much care that consequently necessitated a great amount of manual labour.

In his occupation John was exposed to many hazards, for example, chemical agents, that are recognised today but were not then. Consequently, there was not the same protection offered by health and safety regulations as prevails today. Although during most of his working life he was exposed to significant occupational hazards he did not succumb to them apparently.

John and Ann Margaret had nine children between 1865 and 1883, two of whom died in childhood. This fact is unremarkable. There was a high mortality rate of children under ten years during the 1800s in Scotland. The infectious diseases, tuberculosis, typhus, scarlet fever, whooping cough, diphtheria, measles, and smallpox were the killers. Acquaintance with the death of infants and young children was therefore an inescapable fact of Scottish working class life in this period. In addition to their own children, John and Ann

Margaret took parental responsibility for two of Ann Margaret's siblings, Alexander and Jessie, when they were orphaned in 1863.

For John's children, the main opportunities for employment in Arbroath, although declining, were in the textile industry and most of them became employees of this industry.

All the children had left home by 1907 when Ann Margaret died. John was not on his own for long, because his eldest daughter Helen and her two children joined him. Helen was widowed in 1909 and returned to Arbroath from Dalry, Ayrshire, where she and her husband had lived after their marriage in 1889. In Arbroath she resumed her occupation of canvas weaver. At the age of sixty nine in 1911, John was still working as a bleacher. Without the income from his job, he faced poverty. However, in the following year his retirement from work may have been permitted because at the age of seventy he became eligible for the means tested state pension which had been introduced by law in 1908. At the very end of his life, John lived with his son, James and daughter-in-law. He died in 1916.

Chapter 5

Red Lichtie

This chapter describes the life of James Guthrie Smith, whose paternal family history was described in chapter 4. Because he was born and brought up in Arbroath, he warrants description as a red lichtie, the local nickname for an inhabitant of the town. He also warrants the description of red lichtie or red light, figuratively, for his commitment to egalitarian political change. He was a shoe clicker who worked in Arbroath, Glasgow and Dundee and was twice made unemployed. He was an active supporter of the National Union of Boot and Shoe Operatives (NUBSO), the Independent Labour Party (ILP) and the Arbroath Proletarian Sunday School. He was exempted from conscription during WW1 and was opposed to the War. In his later years, necessity obliged him to earn his living as a tallyman.

James Guthrie Smith was born in 1879 in St Vigeans, Arbroath, when the town had a population of twenty thousand. The town grew considerably during the industrial revolution. He was born at 26 Robert Street, the border between a residential district and the industrial centre of Arbroath. At the southern end of Robert Street was the Spink Street Mill (Flax and Jute Spinning) and beyond the northern end of Robert Street was the Westburn Works for Flax and Hemp Spinning and Weaving. Railway lines, a goods station, a passenger station and other industrial premises were in the vicinity of Robert Street which later acquired a coal depot, sheds, stables, an office and a shop with cellars.

James was born in a two roomed house, one of six owned by a blacksmith, David Christie, who also lived in the street. The neighbouring households were headed by mill workers, flax dressers, a baker, a vintner, a fireman, and a librarian. James lived in Robert Street until the family moved house in 1894, soon after he had left one of Arbroath's ten schools. Because of the provisions for 'half-time work', James's first experience of work may have been a part-time job whilst he was a school pupil.

When James left school, most employment in Arbroath was in the textile and allied industries. James's family earned their living from these industries. However, the textile industry was in decline from about 1880 and the boot and shoe industry was of rising importance in the town. Tanning and shoe making had a history in Arbroath that went back to the 1700s and it expanded very much in the late 1800s in the form of two well-known major firms. These were Colin Grant, founded in 1862 with a new factory that opened in 1882 and Samuel Fairweather, in business from 1857. James found employment in the boot and shoe industry in Arbroath as a clicker.

The boot and shoe industry went through much change in the late 1800s. Mechanisation and a new division of labour undermined the tradition of craftsmen who had served an apprenticeship, solely carrying out all the processes of shoe making. In the new division of labour, clickers were employed to cut out the leather for the different parts that made up the shoe or boot. The job was named from the noise that came at the end of the cutting process when the operator's knife hit the cutting board. In larger factories there were many hand-clickers in close proximity to each other; hence there would be many clicks per second. The trade was skilled because it was the clicker's responsibility to maximise the number of uppers which could be cut from skins of leather. They were expected to avoid any thin and damaged areas and to incorporate the (unseen) 'lines' of stretch and resistance which naturally occurred in leather according to the style and construction of the particular shoe. The clicker was considered as the most skilled trade in the industry and was paid on time rates whereas the other trades were paid on piece rates. Boys and youths were recruited to the industry to specialize in cutting leather. After a few months of practice and experience of leather cutting the new recruits to the industry acquired the job description of clicker or to those outside the industry, shoe-clicker.

As a clicker, James became of member of trade union that represented his trade. Employees of the boot and shoe industry in Arbroath were represented by a national trade union that had been formed in 1874 and was called the National Union of Boot and Shoe Operatives from 1898. The formation of the union was the result of a conference held in Northampton by twenty five representatives from branches of an existing union in the shoe making trade that included Arbroath. The purpose of the union was to defend the rights of workers in the boot and shoe making industry. It took up the cause of workers locked out for wanting to join a union and dealt with disputes with employers over working practices. The Arbroath branch flourished with a membership of three hundred and forty five in 1891. In 1912, membership was two hundred and five, and in 1922, four hundred and thirty. NUBSO was one of the largest trade unions in Arbroath, with only the Mill and Factory Workers Union larger. In fact, at the end of the 1800s there was a thriving labour movement in Arbroath that was commensurate with the industrialisation that had occurred in the town. The separate trade unions came together in 1889 to form the Arbroath United Trade Council. Its membership included unions representing engineers, moulders, blacksmiths, printers, joiners, slaters, shoemakers, bakers, general labourers, flaxdressers and mill and factory workers.

James's trade union membership may have been encouraged by the example of his father. For trade unionism was supported by workers in the Arbroath textile industry, one union being the

Arbroath Mill, Factory and Bleachfield Workers' Union. In 1890 in Arbroath, there was a one day strike of bleachers at one of the town's bleachfields.

In addition to his membership of NUBSO, James joined the Independent Labour Party which he supported throughout his life.

The Independent Labour Party (ILP) was founded in 1893 as a national organisation at a conference in Bradford, attended by about one hundred and twenty delegates from various local labour and socialist organisations. The ILP's objective was the establishment of a Socialist Commonwealth, a classless society with all economic resources communally owned and controlled. Its aim was to replace the capitalist system in Britain and also to co-operate with workers in other countries for the same end. According to one historian, those who joined the party as ordinary rank and file members joined a close-knit band of enthusiasts, a harbinger of the new society and the vanguard of the left.

The ILP was one of the bodies which created in 1900, the Labour Representation Committee that became the Labour Party. The ILP remained an important force within the Labour Party until the mid-1920s. Before 1918 the Labour Party had little local organisation and Labour supporters tended to join their local ILP branch. Many prominent Labour MPs between 1900 and 1924 were also ILP members. They included James Ramsay MacDonald and Philip Snowden.

In 1893, the inaugural meeting of a branch of the Independent Labour Party was held in Arbroath. It was chaired by Mr H. McArthur of the Bakers Union and addressed by Miss Stacy B.A. A later public meeting in Arbroath in 1894 was addressed by Ben Tillett (union leader and later Labour MP) on the House of Lords and Trade Unionism. In 1897, the ILP sponsored a lecture by Tom Mann who spoke on the organization of the workers. Tom Mann was a union leader and ILP general secretary for two years who broke with it for the Communist party in later years. In 1908,

Keir Hardie MP, chairman of the Parliamentary Labour Party, campaigned in Arbroath.

James left Arbroath as a young man and was working in his trade in Glasgow in 1901. The boot and shoe trade in Arbroath was prospering at this time shown by a reduction in hours granted to employees in 1899. Therefore, if James had not been obliged to seek work in Glasgow, he may have decided to broaden his horizons and develop his independence by moving there. Of course, the city may have offered even better pay to clickers than Arbroath. Glasgow was an impressive place at the end of the 1800s. It was ranked as one of the finest and richest cities in Europe and acclaimed as a model of organised industrial society. It was unquestionably the 'Second City of the Empire' with an attraction for those living outside it.

James lived as a boarder at 41 Main Street, Bridgeton, in the household headed by Morag Walker, a forty eight-year old a widow from Aberdeenshire who was reliant on boarders for her income. The rest of the household comprised the two daughters of Morag Walker. Sophia Walker, aged twenty three, who helped to keep the house and Bessie Walker, aged twenty one, who was employed as a cotton winder. The remaining member of the household was another boarder, Sydney Judd, a twenty two year old Englishman, also a clicker.

Bridgeton was at the heart of Glasgow's manufacturing industry, with textiles and engineering as important. One employer was W. & J. Martin, leather merchants, tanners and footwear manufacturers. The firm (which had begun in the 1830s) acquired further premises in Bridgeton at Baltic Street in 1901. The Baltic Street premises were less than a mile from 41 Main Street, a distance of about seventeen minutes to walk on foot.

Although Bridgeton later became a bastion of the ILP when James Maxton was elected its member of parliament, at the time James lived there, the ILP was not yet a noticeable political force in the constituency.

James did not stay in Glasgow for long but moved to Dundee where shoe making was an important industry, with thirteen boot and shoe manufacturers in 1904. There may have been a decline of work for clickers in Glasgow or he may have become disillusioned with the city if his residence there had exposed him to its face of urban squalor, sickness and crime.

In Dundee, James met Agnes Murie Fenwick, a leather machinist employed in the same industry as him. They were married in 1906 and lived only few doors away from Agnes's parents. Between 1906 and 1914 they became the parents of five children, one of whom died in infancy. James's first sojourn in Dundee was in a period when the ILP enjoyed increasing support with members successful in elections at the municipal level. Indeed Dundee and Arbroath were the twin centres of active support in the Angus Federation of the ILP. James and Agnes left Dundee for Arbroath in 1907 but returned to the city in 1922.

When James and Agnes moved to Arbroath, better prospects for work and family ties were probably the impetus. Soon after they had moved to Arbroath, James's mother, Ann McLean died in November 1907. In 1909, Agnes's parents left Dundee to become members of their daughter's household. Perhaps, they were finding it difficult to make ends meet as tenants, but as boarders in their daughter's household, they could do so. It is also possible that in their senior years, they were in need of the practical support that James and Agnes could offer them. Had James and Agnes not been hospitable, her parents may have faced the workhouse. Agnes's mother and father stayed with their daughter and son-in-law until their deaths in 1911 and 1913, respectively. Agnes maintained contact with her siblings in Dundee. On Census night 1911, her sister, Elizabeth now married, was a visitor, accompanied by her three-year old daughter, Agnes. In 1915, James's father, John, became a member of the household of James and Agnes until his death in 1916.

From 1914 James and Agnes lived in St Mary Street Arbroath. The street was mainly residential with a few shops, one of which was an Arbroath High Street Coop shop. The principles of the Coop were much admired by James and so he was probably a regular customer. The Coop may have helped James and Agnes to manage their money for in Arbroath they had one income to provide for the whole household which comprised two adults and four children. In their early days there, they had family boarders also.

In Arbroath, James's employer was Colin Grant. Colin Grant's firm specialised in boots for agricultural workers and had won gold medals for excellence at the international exhibition for industry, science and art at Edinburgh in 1886 and 1890.

The Arbroath branch of the National Union of Boot and Shoe Operatives of which James was a member, held regular meetings. Meetings considered matters such as compensation for an injured 'shop-mate' and appointment of delegates to the TUC, the General Federation of Trade Unions and the Labour Party Conference. The union had shop clerks rather than shop stewards and members were known as shop mates. James Smith was a shop clerk.

At the September meeting in 1911, a talk was given about the newly established employment exchange by the manager who encouraged members to use it when they were out of work. At several meetings there was discussion of the new National Insurance Act. The Act introduced compulsory contributions for workers that conferred entitlement to unemployment and sickness benefits.

At a number of meetings, disagreements with the employer, Samuel Fairweather, were discussed and in November 1912 there was a stoppage of work there. Disagreements between the union and the employer, Colin Grant, were rarer it seems.

The *Daily Citizen* was launched by the Labour Party and Trades Union Congress as a Labour newspaper in 1912. It did not last for long because popular support instead was given to the initially unofficial *Daily Herald*, launched at the same time. During its launch year, the Arbroath branch was asked by the *Daily Citizen* newspaper to form a circulation committee to get subscriptions for the paper. James was a member of the committee appointed to the task. In 1913, at a branch meeting, criticism was expressed of the executive committee of the union for insufficient support being given to the *Daily Citizen* newspaper. The *Daily Herald* survived to become the *Sun* decades later.

At a meeting, in February 1913 there was discussion of the board of arbitration for the industry and an offer in respect of a minimum wage.

At its meeting in September 1913, the branch received a circular from the ILP urging support for a resolution to condemn the Lord Lieutenant of Ireland and others for their brutal suppression of public meetings in Dublin. This circular referred to public meetings held in support of a general strike in Dublin which started in August. The meetings were officially prohibited and there were ensuing demonstrations, protests and violence.

In 1915, the branch organised a special meeting for women members and considered a strike over the employment of non-union women at Samuel Fairweather.

In 1916 concern was expressed at the branch about non-union membership locally and efforts were made to recruit non-members at Colin Grant without success initially.

An indication of the mood of the branch was shown by the meeting in January 1917. James Stalker (an ILP officer and shop mate of James at Colin Grant), moved a resolution to condemn officials of the Seamen's and Firemen's Union for their actions in stopping Messrs Ramsay MacDonald and Jowett proceeding to Petrograd. The Seamen's and Firemen's Union was pro-war and had instructed members to refuse to work any ship on which Messrs. Ramsay Macdonald and Jowett, 'the peace propagandists' might to sail. MacDonald and Jowett were ILP members of parliament, who were anti-war and were seeking to bring an end to it through international negotiations in Petrograd and Stockholm. The resolution was defeated by twenty two votes to seventeen, which showed the support in the branch for and against the war. It was indicative of the wider division of opinion in trade unions in Scotland over the war.

In 1918, James was unanimously appointed treasurer of the branch. The union nationally had one hundred thousand members by 1920 but years later the membership fell which necessitated it amalgamating with other trade unions in 1971.

Concurrent with his membership of NUBSO, James was a committed member of the Independent Labour Party in Arbroath. As a member of the ILP, James supported his party's policy towards World War One. The ILP was stringently opposed to the First World War and was the main anti-war political organisation in Britain. In that respect, it differed from the Labour party which was committed to supporting the war effort. As a result, tensions persisted between the two for the duration of the war. The ILP was largely united in its opposition to the war although there was a spectrum of attitudes within it. For some, the war was opposed on Christian grounds that violence and taking life was unjustified. For others, the War was irrational and a failure of diplomacy and for others still, particularly the Scottish division of the ILP, the war was considered a product of capitalism with both sides equally to blame. Members taking the latter view were willing to fight but only in defence of socialism. Their opposition was to a war which they believed could only mean workers killing each other in the millions in the interests of their bosses.

Outside the broad unity of the party, some members supported the war. It was estimated by one respected ILP anti-war insider that about a fifth of the membership deviated from Party policy and supported the war. In its opposition to the war, the ILP strongly opposed the introduction of conscription and maintained it was a fatal infringement of civil liberties. With other organisations such as the No-Conscription Fellowship, the ILP distributed leaflets and held meetings that roundly condemned the idea of a British conscript army. Those opposed to the war like the ILP, were subject to much public hostility. The ultra-patriotic opinion of the time incited the giving of white feathers to shame men who were not in uniform. James wholly supported ILP policy on World War One on the grounds that it was an outcome of capitalism to which he was opposed. As a free thinker, religious beliefs did not inspire his opposition to the war.

In opposing World War One, James was a dissident from mainstream opinion that was militantly pro-war. Those who opposed the war and supported peace with Germany could encounter hostility from the public at large. The hostility could take the form of petty verbal abuse or on occasion, assault in the street. Pacifists could be thrown into jail for the most trivial of reasons. In the early months of the war, ILP members were frequently attacked and beaten up. On one occasion during the war, James, because of his opposition to the war, was beaten up by a group of men.

The prosecution of the War led to the introduction of conscription in 1916. Military Service Acts of that year made all British men liable for compulsory military service. At first the law applied only to unmarried men but soon it was extended to all men of military age (18 to 41) including those who were married unless they possessed a certificate of exemption. Local Military Service Tribunals were formed across Britain (over two thousand) to consider applications for exemption. Separate tribunals were established to consider appeals. In 1916, James was thirty seven years old and so became liable for conscription. Only a certificate of exemption granted by a local Military Service Tribunal could excuse him from service.

Exemptions could be asked for on four grounds: medical unfitness or infirmity; exceptional business or personal circumstances (such as the potential collapse of an applicant's business, or the applicant's responsibility for caring for elderly relatives); conscientious objection; work of national importance. Exemptions could be granted as absolute, conditional or temporary.

James was not conscripted for military service in World War One because he was granted exemption although records have not survived that show the grounds for exemption. The most probable grounds for James's exemption from conscription were that his work was of national importance. For he enjoyed good health, had no exceptional business or personal reasons to be exempted, nor was he known to have converted his opposition to the war to conscientious objection. A local newspaper, *The Arbroath* Guide, reported the sittings of the Arbroath Burgh Military Tribunal between May 1916 and August 1918 and many exemptions were granted to shoe clickers. Appeals were made by the boot and shoe manufacturers or individual employees. At one sitting, the employer Samuel Fairweather supported the application for exemption made by a clicker and asserted that the applicant was in one of the key positions in the factory and if such men were to be taken away, it would be impossible to supply the boots necessary for the Government. At another sitting the employer Colin Grant appeared on behalf of his son, Colin, who was engaged in business with him at his boot and shoe factory. He said that the firm was over- head and ears with government work and it was very strenuous indeed. It was unanimously agreed by the Tribunal to allow continued conditional exemption to Colin Grant.

Of course, James's application for exemption may never have appeared at a hearing for applications were at times agreed by Tribunals without the necessity of a hearing. It was evident that the boot and shoe manufacturers in Arbroath during World War One were very busy delivering contracts made with the Government to supply the Armed Forces. In meeting these contracts, the boot and shoe manufacturers were engaged in work of national importance. Clickers were a highly skilled occupation in the manufacture of boots and were in short supply because of the War. Replacement of them was difficult for employers to arrange. Without them, the nationally important task of production of boots for the armed forces was jeopardised. It was necessary therefore for clickers to be granted conditional exemption from military service in Arbroath. Conditional exemption meant that the exemption was given as long as the condition did not change. The condition for these applicants was that they remained working as clickers. In granting exemptions, the Arbroath Burgh Military Tribunal exercised its judicial independence. It seems that if exemptions had not been granted, then satisfactory substitutes for experienced clickers could not have been secured rapidly to maintain the supply of army boots need to successfully prosecute the war.

Therefore, it seems that James as a clicker, secured exemption from military service during World War One on grounds of his work being of national importance. Because he remained in the job of clicker throughout the war, his exemption was never withdrawn.

As one of those who were exempted from military service, James was one of many. For over seven hundred thousand men applied for exemption and it has been estimated that as many men were exempted from military service in World War One as served overseas with the British army.

Of the period in which James was a member of the Arbroath ILP, records for some of the time have survived and they show that he was a stalwart of the branch. Membership of the branch ranged between forty and sixty, with attendance at meetings fluctuating between six and thirty eight. In 1920 he was minutes secretary. He served as chair for some meetings in 1921. In 1921 he was one of the three members who constituted the election committee that made a report to a branch meeting. In 1922, he was elected auditor. He took part in business meetings and also in campaigning. Business matters included for example, the organisation of a social with a prize draw and tea to be provided by West Port Coop Society.

Branch meetings between 1920 and 1922 considered transactions with the Trades Council, the Montrose Burghs Labour Party, the Angus ILP Federation and attendance at the Proletarian/Socialist Sunday School. Other matters considered were receipt of a circular of National Hands off Russia, promotion of the *Daily Herald* and the appointment of delegates to a Scottish Temperance Conference.

An illustration of the opinion of the branch was shown at a meeting in December 1921, which passed a resolution in support of John McLean. John Mclean was a revolutionary republican socialist who had been imprisoned for his opposition to World War One. In September 1921, he made a speech at an open air meeting in Glasgow in which he suggested that the unemployed should just take food rather than starve. He was arrested, charged with sedition, tried and found guilty. He was sentenced to one year's imprisonment and was released in 1922. The branch clearly had great sympathy for him making a huge personal sacrifice for the humanitarian cause that he believed in. Popular support for John McLean was also shown because he was seen as a victim of persecution by the Establishment.

Prominent members of the ILP visited Arbroath to speak at meetings and James was amongst those members who provided hospitality to them in their homes. One prominent member of the ILP and visitor to Arbroath was James Maxton. Maxton was adopted in 1914, as parliamentary candidate for the constituency of which Arbroath was a part, Montrose Burghs. He was a pacifist and campaigned against Britain's involvement in the World War One and against the introduction of conscription. Maxton was imprisoned in 1916 for delivering pro-strike speeches at a demonstration to oppose the Munitions Act. He was elected as Member of Parliament for Glasgow, Bridgeton in 1922.

Another visitor to Arbroath was Mrs Philip Snowden. She was a campaigner for women's suffrage and temperance and wife of an ILP leader. She addressed a meeting in January 1920. The title of her talk was, 'Who is to blame for starving Europe?' The meeting was attended by four hundred people and when it had ended, a collection was taken for Save the Children Fund. In commenting on the Russian revolution Mrs Snowden was quoted as saying 'What caused the revolution was that when the people got the fumes of liquor out of their brains, they would not stand the tyrannies of that country.' Her comment is indicative of the widespread popular support in the ILP for the 1917 revolution in Russia and also for temperance. James may have supported the temperance movement early in his life but in his later years he freely consumed alcohol.

An offshoot of the ILP in Arbroath was the Proletarian Sunday School and James was its Secretary between 1920 and 1922. Its meetings were held every Sunday at 2.30 p.m. James and his children attended these meetings which were not always well supported. At Arbroath ILP branch meetings, reference was usually made to the Socialist Sunday School rather than the Proletarian Sunday School. So there was ambiguity about the exact title of the School as far as its supporters were concerned. Although no records of the Arbroath Proletarian or Socialist Sunday School have survived, historical sources are informative about the broader movement of which it was part. In Scotland, the Socialist Sunday School movement began in Glasgow in the 1890s, but soon spread to other parts of the country. The aim was to promote and share socialist values, and to offer an alternative to the teaching of Christian Sunday schools and state schools. The movement flourished until the 1930s, and was closely linked with the Independent Labour Party.

In many respects, the Socialist Sunday School meetings were run along similar lines to church Sunday schools and services. They had a set order, and included lessons, recitation of texts, a collection which was given to a chosen charity or fund, and hymns. The movement also organised a range of social activities for members, including parties, outings, picnics, and fêtes.

Unlike the church Sunday schools, the Socialist Sunday School meetings were attended by people of all ages. The movement offered secular alternatives to christenings, marriage, and funerals and therefore appealed to freethinkers who were sceptical of religious beliefs, of which James was one.

The key values that underpinned the Socialist Sunday Schools were love, justice, learning, social responsibility and the dignity of labour. In promoting these principles, the Schools sought to ensure that children would become capable and responsible thinkers.

The Proletarian Sunday Schools were run on a similar basis to the Socialist Sunday Schools but with the emphasis on the teachings of Marx and revolutionary Socialism. At their peak of popularity in the early 1920s, these schools had over thirty branches in cities and towns throughout Scotland and several in England. The Proletarian Sunday Schools had much in common with the Socialist Sundays Schools but differed in being more militant and anti-clerical.

The establishment of Proletarian Sunday schools in Scotland is credited to the political campaigner who founded them from 1918, Tom Anderson. Initially, Tom Anderson founded Socialist Sunday Schools from 1894 but after he had joined the Socialist Labour Party in 1910 his political outlook changed and he promoted Proletarian Sunday Schools instead.

The ambiguous identity of the Arbroath Proletarian Sunday School was probably because it depended on the support of socialists who were not members of the ILP. Amongst the political parties in Arbroath was a branch of the Socialist Labour Party, the secretary of which was James Turnbull. He was the husband of Mrs Turnbull, the treasurer of the Proletarian Sunday School.

When James informed his ILP branch in 1922 that he was to leave Arbroath for Dundee he was thanked by the Secretary, on behalf of the branch for his past services as an active member who held various offices.

James and Agnes left Arbroath for Dundee in 1922 because James lost his job as a clicker and there was little prospect of getting another one in the town. In 1920, his employer, Colin Grant, encountered difficulties because of a fall in demand and later closed down. The industry was in decline nationally, for the extension and improvement of machinery had raised output per operative but domestic consumption of foot wear failed to increase by the same proportion. Many employers kept on their books more employees than they really needed with the consequence that work had to be shared. Sharing of work resulted in reduced pay. From his past experience, James knew that Dundee offered better prospects for him as a clicker than Arbroath and so he and Agnes moved back there.

After Colin Grant's factory closed, it was unused, and then became the Marine Ballroom and later a bus depot. It was listed as a historic building in 2000 when it was considered an important example of Victorian industrial architecture. In 2008, it was converted into flats.

In Dundee, James found work in his occupation, but earnings were still modest in relation to household needs. Although in one of the better paid jobs in the shoe industry, he and Agnes were unable to afford to pay for the cost of a school uniform so his son Stewart, was not allowed to progress to a grammar school when it offered a place. James and Agnes lived in Downfield, a village in Angus, not long included within the Dundee city boundaries and therefore not yet part of the urban life of the city that had absorbed it. In Downfield, James was employed at the Angus Shoe Works Ltd which also had premises in central Dundee. The Downfield premises were near to James's house. During the General Strike in May 1926, James was on strike. His NUBSO branch gave its support for the General Strike by an unofficial stoppage of work. Nationally, the NUBSO was not required by the TUC to call out its members and instead gave strong support for the strike through supplying funds to the miners. However, some branches wished to show greater solidarity and did so by striking. The response to the general strike by trade unions was complicated and uneven as a result of the guidance given by the TUC and the differing views throughout the trade union movement.

James became unemployed when the Downfield premises of the Angus Shoe Works Ltd closed in 1931. Boot and shoe industries had developed in countries that were previously good markets for British products and there was a fall in sales to these countries which had also introduced tariff barriers. In 1931, the great slump occurred which meant there was economic contraction, high unemployment and severity in public spending. In Scotland, the slump of 1931-33 put more than a quarter of the work force, out of a job. The shoe making industry in Dundee had contracted to six employers in 1931 and its contraction continued in subsequent years. James was unable to find a job in his usual trade.

When James became unemployed he became eligible for cash help from the state in the form of public assistance. But to qualify for public assistance as an unemployed man, he was subject to the household means test introduced in 1931. As such there was an inspection by a government official to make sure that the claimant had no hidden earnings or savings, undisclosed source(s) of income or other means of support. For many claimants this was a humiliating experience and was much resented. In retrospect, the household means test required claimants to prove just how poor they were, in intimate domestic detail. The means test imposed form-filling, impertinent questions, and regular, shamingly visible, visits from investigators licensed to peer into cooking-pots, rule that one chair per person was enough, and order claimants to sell their spare blankets. By the time he was in receipt of public assistance, two of James's children were married and had left home, whilst two remained. On occasion, the youngest, George, who was employed as an apprentice joiner, absented himself from home to conceal one source of the household's meagre income. His absence was an attempt to alleviate the harshness of the means test.

In Dundee, James maintained his vocal support for the ILP. The party increasingly distanced itself from the Labour party on many policy issues from the 1920s, the Labour Party committing itself to gradualism and moderation and the ILP working towards 'Socialism Now'. The leaders, Snowden and MacDonald, left the ILP, in 1928 and 1930 respectively. The ILP disillusioned with the Labour Party, dis-affiliated from it in 1932, which led to a sharp fall in ILP membership across the country and the closure of many branches. The party declined in Dundee and by 1941 it was no longer listed in the *Dundee Directory*. The contraction of the ILP was hastened by the growing influence of its rivals, the Labour party and the Communist party. It fell into their shadows. The last member of parliament elected for the ILP was in 1946. In 1975 the ILP ceased to be the Independent Labour Party (ILP) and reconstituted itself as Independent Labour Publications (ILP) a political pressure group, combining a parliamentary and extra- parliamentary perspectives for democratic social change.

After several years of unemployment, James found work and in 1937 he was a credit draper's collector or salesman collector. In his new job, sometimes described as a tallyman, he collected weekly payments on a door to door basis from households which had bought clothing or fabrics on credit. Sales of these items were also sometimes a responsibility of the job. This job was very different from the skilled and socially co-operative occupation of clicker. It was not a job of his choosing but there were no vacancies for clickers, the shoe making industry being in the doldrums. So necessity compelled him to take a job with a better income than reliance on public assistance. He was still a tallyman in 1940 when Agnes died but he later retired from the job. Long after he had lost his job as a clicker James still possessed a collection of tools of his former trade which he put to use to make or mend shoes for the family. As a widower, he enjoyed meeting friends regularly in the pub and relied on the hospitality of the families of his children. He died in 1946.

Chapter 6

Highland Line

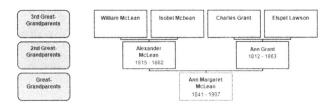

In geographical terms, the Highlands are the part of Scotland north-west of the Highland Boundary Fault which crosses mainland Scotland whilst the Lowlands are the area south of the Fault. An important distinction in the history of Scotland is between the Highlands and the Lowlands. This distinction was based on language as well as culture. However, these differences narrowed over time. The differences between highlanders and lowlanders prompted some mutual antipathy at one time and later became merely a source of banter. The maternal forebears of James Guthrie Smith came from the Highlands and this chapter gives an account of their lives.

The lives of three maternal forebears, in direct order of descent, are profiled. Elspeth Lawson was born in the late 1700s in the rural parish of Cromdale, Inverness-shire and married Charles Grant. Her daughter, Ann born in 1812, married Alexander MacLean from the rural parish of Moy, Inverness-shire. They migrated from the Highlands to the Arbroath area, where he worked as an agricultural labourer, then a railway labourer. Ann's daughter, Ann Margaret, born in 1841 worked as a farm servant in the Arbroath area before marrying John Smith. Ann Margaret and John became the parents of James Guthrie Smith in 1879.

Elspeth Lawson

The earliest known maternal forebear of James Guthrie Smith was Elspeth Lawson, born in the parish of Cromdale, Inverness-shire. The birth of a child named Elspeth Lawson occurred in Cromdale in 1766 and in 1782. Unfortunately, a paucity of information about these births does not make it possible to identify exactly which one was the maternal forebear of James Guthrie Smith. Nevertheless, the church registers do confirm that the maternal ancestry of James Guthrie Smith originated in Cromdale, in the Highlands. How far back in Cromdale's history James Smith's maternal ancestry lies has to remain a matter of conjecture. It is valid to assume that his early maternal ancestors were from the Highlands, if not from the parish of Cromdale.

In the late 1700s, the parish of Cromdale was wholly agricultural and in the solitary ownership of Sir James Grant. This inland parish was about thirty six miles south east of the town of Inverness. The population was largely peasant and Gaelic speaking with most able to understand and speak English. The population numbered about three thousand people. Oats, barley, rye, wheat, turnips and potatoes were grown and sheep and cattle were raised. There were fir plantations that necessitated forestry work. Many left the parish to work on roads and other public works in the summer.

The physical environment of Cromdale parish was characteristically Highland: there were hills, forests of pine, larch and oak and lakes which supported commensurate wildlife (grouse and white hare for example). The river Spey, in which there was salmon, ran through the parish in a half moon. The parish was well above sea level and offered a healthy climate. Peat was freely available as the fuel for cooking and heating. The cultivated land in the parish was barely a tenth of the total, with the greatest acreage being hills, moors and mosses.

Elspeth Lawson's early life was in a society in transition. In origin, it was a tribal, peasant society based on the clan. Membership of a clan entailed various social obligations but most importantly, land was in the ownership of the chief who leased it to a hierarchy of tenants. The tenants and sub-tenants numbering eight to twelve lived in group settlements for joint farming. Land was divided into strips by the system of run-rig so that even those peasants at the bottom of the hierarchy of land tenure, (cottars), had at least small pieces of land for themselves. The group settlements farmed for household subsistence and to pay the rent.

Elspeth's life as a female in her father's peasant household can be imagined from historical accounts. Peasant households commonly had a strip or more of land to cultivate. Families in peasant husbandry lived in small huts with turf roofs and a central fire in the middle of the floor and livestock wandered in and out. In the winter, farms could get cut off by blizzards. In summer, the community moved up to the hill shielings and lived in temporary huts. The essentials of life were fashioned from local materials. Therefore, clothing was spun and woven from animal hair and brogues were cut from skin. Many peasants had but a subsistence existence and were heavily reliant on potatoes. Highland life was primitive and grim.

Important changes occurred in the Highlands after 1760 (and continued throughout much of the 1800s). The land owners deciding that there was a better future for them in replacing peasant husbandry by a commercial agricultural system based on expansion in the production of commodities for sale to the rest of Britain. In pursuit of their goals, the landowners, who were often clan chiefs, consolidated land into single tenant farms. Many of these farms were intended for sheep. Joint farms and the run-rig system were abolished where possible. As a consequence of these changes, new separate holdings of land were created from separate strips and many peasants became landless. They became either farm servants with yearly contracts with a tenant farmer or labourers with small pieces of land and working on an irregular basis for farmers. Those who held onto land were frequently obliged to move out to the periphery of fertile areas. Because of the expansion of population that occurred concurrently with the tenancy consolidation, there was an even greater fragmentation of land holdings so many tenants came to hold very small pieces of land in crowded conditions – the crofters.

Unlike many Highland parishes, Cromdale had a sole landowner who adopted a strategy for agricultural improvement that assumed a future for all inhabitants. He created the solitary village in the parish, Grantown in 1776, to promote manufacturing and trade so that tenants displaced by agricultural reform were rehoused and provided with a different means of livelihood. In the village, a range of artisans lived and sold their services, linen was produced from locally grown flax and there were two parochial schools. The pursuit of agricultural reforms in the Highlands varied from place to place and it appears that in Cromdale they were managed without brutal clearances and evictions. The landowner apparently acted from enlightened self-interest. Nonetheless, the consolidation of tenancies that occurred in Cromdale, transformed the way of life as it did in the rest of the Highlands.

Elspeth married Charles Grant, just before the turn of the century, it seems, (the church registers for marriage in Cromdale have survived only from 1798). They became the parents of four children between 1804 and 1812. Their lives were directly affected by the war with France between 1793 and 1815 for Charles was enlisted into the Inverness-shire militia and became a corporal. Cromdale was a largely peasant community and the lower strata of such communities were an important source of recruitment for the militia. Therefore, Charles, was probably a labourer with a small plot of land. Agricultural labourers were able to easily combine their paid work which was on a daily or weekly basis, with their part-time military service. In their absence, any plot of land for domestic cultivation could be managed by their families.

There was not a significant division of labour in peasant households between men and women in the Highlands which suggests that in Charles's absence on militia service, Elspeth extended her usual role by greater outdoor activity on their own plot of land. The militia service boosted the household income of recruits by payments made for each day of service and by dependant allowances paid for children. The records suggest that Charles was a militiaman for eight years and perhaps longer. As compulsory service was for five years, he may have volunteered for additional years because of the cash that it brought to the household.

Ann Grant

Ann Grant, the daughter of Elspeth and Charles, was born in 1812 in Cromdale where she spent her early years and started her working life as a servant on a farm. Her work may have included both labouring in the fields and domestic work. In Cromdale, opportunities for work remained wholly in agriculture other than for a few shops and businesses in Grantown serving the local population. The parish, encouraged by the sole landowner, had undergone much change in its agriculture by the time Ann had reached adulthood. The solitary landowner, the Earl of Seafield, acted with civic responsibility as had his kinsman and predecessor. A hospital was built in 1824, more schools created, roads and farm buildings kept in good condition. Modern methods, such as crop rotation, were employed in agriculture and sheep and cattle were still reared in the parish. Cromdale was in the part of eastern Inverness-shire where improvements were made successfully to secure stability and prosperity.

In 1839, twenty six year old Ann married twenty three year old Alexander McLean. He was a native of the Inverness-shire parish of Moy and Dalarossie, about twenty five miles to the west of Cromdale and populated by about a thousand inhabitants. One of seven siblings, and the son of a labourer, he had migrated to Cromdale. Like Ann he was employed on a farm but not the same one as her. Moy and Dalarossie, which included Loch Moy, was wholly agricultural but because it was wild and mountainous, only a small proportion of it was cultivated. It had no towns or villages and the people were Gaelic Speaking.

The parish of Moy and Dalarossie was in the ownership of several proprietors, some of whom were absentee landlords. There had been little encouragement from them for the adoption of modern methods of farming. They had instituted clearance, and a consolidation of tenancies. Sheep farming had been extended on a large scale and tenants and sub-tenants displaced. The land owners were indifferent to plight of the inhabitants, many of who lived in poverty or were forced to migrate to other parts of the country or overseas. The tipping point for Alexander may have been around 1836-1837 for a crop failure occurred in these years causing great destitution throughout much of the Highlands. Migration became a necessity for many to survive. Cromdale seems to have been spared this disaster and its good fortune may have been known by Alexander when he decided to leave Moy and Dalarossie.

Unmarried farm workers were preferred in Cromdale and much of the surrounding region. It was customary for young, single, male and female farm servants to be accommodated within the farmer's household, eating in a kitchen and sleeping in an attic or outhouse of the farm itself. Therefore, the opportunities for being hired for farm service were reduced for Ann and Alexander after their marriage in 1839 in Cromdale. The option of renting a cottage and smallholding in Cromdale and being hired for casual labouring may not have been available either. Whatever the reasons, Ann and Alexander left the Highlands after their marriage and moved to the Lowlands in 1840. They found work and accommodation in the Arbroath area of Angus. Arbroath was a journey south east from Cromdale of about a hundred miles. It may not have been the first time that Alexander or Ann had migrated south for it was the custom of many young Highlanders, male and female, (from the age of about fifteen years) to obtain temporary work, often in farms, in the summer in the Lowlands. Therefore, they may well have had prior knowledge of their destination when they left Cromdale.

Angus was one of the eastern counties of Scotland with highly capitalised farms that relied on a large labour force to harvest grain, potato and turnips. These workers were often itinerant workers from the Highlands. Some parts of Angus welcomed married farm workers and provided accommodation for them. Ann and Alexander settled in Angus and became the parents of seven children between 1840 and 1855, two of whom died in childhood.

Initially Alexander and Ann lived in the parish of St Vigeans from 1840 until 1843. Alexander was an agricultural labourer and not a farm servant. Labourers were paid by the day or week and in effect were self-employed whereas farm servants had annual contracts and were employees. Labourers were hired and laid off when necessary. They rented cottages and subsistence plots and their continued occupation of these premises depended upon them paying the rent in cash. Farm workers generally preferred annual contracts because of the certainty of income. Alexander may have been unable to secure a contract because of a lack of skills (for example, experience of working with horses). Labourers in Angus were about a fifth of the total number of farm workers. Although the labourers did not have the certainty of income in Scotland, their weekly rate of pay was better than that of farm servants. In 1841 Alexander and Ann provided lodgings for a young man named Alexander McLean, an agricultural labourer and perhaps a kinsman of Alexander who had followed them south in search of work.

In 1843, Alexander and Ann moved to Inverkeillor, a parish adjacent to Arbroath. In Inverkeillor, they lived in the village of Leysmill where there was a railway station and Alexander forsook agriculture for the railways. He was employed as a railway labourer for the rest of his working life. In 1847 there were forty seven thousand and two hundred and ten railwaymen in the United Kingdom and a quarter of them were labourers. These labourers, unlike those who built the railways, were in stable employment and not party to the navvies' distinct lifestyle of communal living and persistent mobility.

Alexander was employed by the Arbroath to Forfar Railway, a pioneering local railway. The railway had fully opened in January1839 primarily for the transport of freight, especially seaborne coal from Arbroath and quarry stone to Arbroath for onward transportation by sea. Passenger traffic also became an important source of revenue for the railway company.

The Arbroath and Forfar Railway had to make changes to its rail track after 1845 because Parliament had decreed that trunk railways would have to be made to a standard gauge. It had to alter its gauge and to provide a double track. Suitable labour was required to perform this work and Alexander was hired by the Company at this time. In 1848 the Arbroath and Forfar Railway came under the Aberdeen Railway as far as the operation of the line was concerned. In 1856 the Aberdeen Railway merged with the Scottish Midland Junction Railway to become the Scottish North East Railway. These changes may have made little difference to the lives of railway labourers like Alexander even if the changes excited investors.

Whilst records for Alexander's life as a railwayman in the early Victorian era have not survived, historical sources illuminate his life. Employees were commonly recruited locally by the railway companies and agricultural labourers were a main source. For workers like Alexander, railway employment was attractive because the pay was a real improvement on agricultural pay. On average, the weekly wage of a railwayman was several shillings greater than for an agricultural labourer. Additionally, for railwaymen generally, their work for the railway gave them gave them slightly better security of employment. Former agricultural labourers no longer had to seek work on a regular basis but they now had only one week's notice. There was the possibility of payment for overtime and bonuses on occasion too. Railway employees were liable to be moved about and consequently required accommodation. Whilst their family was still small, Alexander and Ann were able use their accommodation for lodgers, from whom they obtained additional income. In 1851, their lodger, Alexander Meechie, was a twenty one year old porter from Aberdeenshire.

As a railwayman, Alexander McLean was one of the permanent waymen, comprising gangers, platelayers and labourers on the Arbroath and Forfar Railway. The task of the permanent waymen was to make sure their section of the line was in safe working order and there was regular daily inspection of their work. Their tools were picks, shovels, hammers, wrenches and track gauges. Gangs of five men were responsible for portions of track of three miles in length and their principal tasks were turning or replacing bad rails, trimming the ballast and repairing the fences. Approaching trains had to be signalled to stop when the rails were being turned or removed. Although careers were made by some railwaymen there were no such opportunities for the permanent waymen. They remained outside the main framework of railway life because of their working location away from stations.

Whilst the wages of a railway labourer were better than those of an agricultural labourer, Alexander became subject to strict discipline that was not characteristic of his previous occupation. Railwaymen were subject to discipline to ensure safety and it was enforced through punishment for misconduct. The most serious misconduct could result in dismissal or prosecution. Railwaymen were required to work long hours with a bare minimum for sleep. There was no statutory ceiling on the hours worked which were frequently fifteen hours a day and eighty eight hours weekly. A seven day week was common. These long hours together with a lack of training contributed to many fatal accidents on the railways. In becoming a railwayman, Alexander was exposed to risks to life and limb that were far greater than for most other workers. Railwaymen were the third most dangerous occupation after mining and the merchant navy. The regulation of health and safety was virtually non-existent in the early Victorian era and there was little protection from trade unions because their organisation in the industry was in an embryonic state. The railway companies were indifferent to the dangers of the industry. As a result, there were many accidents and injuries, not all of which were reported publicly, because there was no obligation to do so.

Whilst most railwaymen's hours were occupied by work, their wives like Ann Grant had all the domestic chores to do which in rural Inverkeillor probably included cultivation of vegetables on a plot of land. There may have been some seasonal work in farming for which she and the children were paid. Living in rural Angus, spinning flax or weaving linen was customary for many wives and so that also may have been amongst her chores that earned cash.

Alexander's railway employment ended in 1862 as a result of his death from compression of the brain. He was aged forty six. Whilst the condition can occur from a variety of causes, a stroke for example, it is most commonly the result of a head injury. As Alexander was in a dangerous occupation and so it is most probable that his premature death resulted from an accident in his job. In an industry whose employees were in greater danger than most other occupations, shunters and permanent waymen were particularly at risk. When statistics were collected and published in the years after Alexander's death, they showed a shocking death toll of railway employees with an average of 682 deaths every year in the 1870s.

For Ann and the rest of the family, much misery and distress can be imagined from Alexander's death. There were no rights to compensation for the railway companies were not compelled by law to make provision. The railway companies usually made small donations, ten pounds for example, to the dependants of men who had fatal accidents at work. These payments were made in part, if not wholly, to reduce the chances of a widow taking legal action for more generous compensation. Funeral expenses were met also and very occasionally a small pension for a few weeks was paid to the dependants. Whatever payments were made to Alexander's family by his employer, they were almost certainly meagre. For these payments were differentiated according to grade, with the smallest amounts given to grades at the bottom of the railway hierarchy. The railway labourers were at the bottom of the hierarchy.

Had Alexander been able to afford membership of a friendly society, (which were promoted by the railway companies to evade their responsibility for compensation), there may have been a lump sum accident death allowance paid but few friendly societies provided widows' pensions. Those in the most dangerous jobs were often not allowed to join a Friendly society because the hazardous nature of their job made the need for pay-outs too likely.

Ann Grant did not survive Alexander very long. She died in 1863 at the age of fifty one. A record of her death has not survived but conjecture suggests that her death may have been from grief. The impact on the children of the early deaths of their parents in close succession can only have been considerable. At the time of the deaths, the two eldest, Ann Margaret and William, had left home. The younger children were still living at home when their mother died: Jessie, fourteen years old, Alexander, ten years old, and James Cameron, seven years old. The family's response to this crisis is described next, under the life of Ann Margaret McLean.

Ann Margaret McLean

Ann Margaret McLean, the daughter of Ann and Alexander, was born 1841 in St Vigeans, on the outskirts of Arbroath and her childhood was spent in rural Inverkeillor where she became a farm servant. In 1861 she was one of seven farm servants employed on an Inverkeillor farm of one hundred and eighty acres. Of the seven, three were young women. Women farm servants might be employed wholly in the fields or to combine outdoor work in the fields with domestic work in the farmhouse. Ann's work appears to have been a combination. Outdoors, the work could include hand-weeding, reaping with the sickle and harvesting the grain. Indoors, the work could include cooking, baking, cleaning, sewing and washing. Women carried out virtually every task on a farm except management of horses.

Women were about a quarter of the regular agricultural labour force in Scotland during Ann's lifetime, in addition to which they were also employed in great numbers on a seasonal, part-time and informal basis. A principal reason for their extensive employment in agriculture in the Lowlands (compared to much of England) was to substitute for a shortage of adult males who had migrated to the expanding manufacturing sector, attracted by the greater financial rewards. However, it was also true that women had long been widely employed on Scottish farms before the rise of manufacturing. Another reason for their extensive employment in agriculture was that their employers paid them about half the wage of men.

Ann was still a farm servant when she married John Smith in 1864. John was employed as a porter at Leysmill station in, Inverkeillor and had formerly been a ploughman in Kincardine.

In 1863, after her father and mother had died, Ann Margaret, and her younger brother William, picked up the pieces of the family that had been broken by the premature deaths of their parents. They divided responsibility between themselves for their orphaned siblings.

William had been apprenticed to a blacksmith in 1861 at the age of fifteen and in 1864 he married Isabella Phillip. He and Isabella assumed responsibility for his younger brother, James Cameron, who at the age of fifteen in 1871 was still part of their household in Inverkeillor. Ann Margaret and her husband assumed responsibility for Alexander and Jessie until they chose to leave. In 1866, Ann Margaret and John left Inverkeillor for Johnshaven in Kincardine-shire as a result of John's employer posting him there.

When Ann Margaret and John assumed responsibility for Jessie after the death of her mother, their responsibility became greater than for her alone. In October 1864, Jessie at the age of fifteen and unmarried gave birth to a son, William. In Scotland, 9% of all births were illegitimate. As the mother of an illegitimate child, Jessie faced a predicament. Although she was of working age, few employers would take on the mother of an illegitimate child as a regular worker because of the distraction from her job of child care and there was also a stigma attached to illegitimacy. Therefore, for an unmarried mother, it was difficult to get a job and care for her child. However, in many rural areas of Scotland where illegitimacy was unexceptional, little popular stigma was attached to extra-marital childbirth. In these circumstances, it was common for the mothers of illegitimate children to live with their parents and support themselves with paid work, frequently as domestic or general servants. After the first year or so, it was also common for many of these children to be looked after by their grandmothers as their mother had left home in order to obtain work further afield, especially in hard times. These unmarried mothers would often send remissions home to their mother for the upkeep of the child. The families of unmarried mothers were expected to shoulder the burden of their daughter's predicament and generally did so.

When Jessie gave birth to her son William, Ann Margaret stepped into the mother's customary role and cared for her younger sister's child, William. She adopted the customary role of the grandmother of an illegitimate child in many rural areas of Scotland. During William's first year, Ann Margaret was free of other child care responsibilities until the birth of her first child, in 1865. That permitted Jessie to find work to support herself and William. When Ann Margaret and John moved to Johnshaven, William accompanied them but Jessie did not. Instead, she decided to remain in the area where she had paid work and could find lodgings relatively easily. She may have sent remissions to Ann

Margaret in Johnshaven to help with William's upkeep. Visits to him may not have been frequent because the distance between Leysmill and Johnshaven was over twenty miles.

When John and Ann Margaret returned to the Arbroath area from Johnshaven, Jessie apparently did not become more involved in the upbringing of her son. William remained in the loving household of Ann Margaret and John, until he left it after 1881. He became a flax dresser, married, and moved with his family to Dundee where he was employed as a van driver.

When her son William was born, Jessie changed her name to Alison, the name by which she was known thereafter. In 1871, Alison was living in lodgings in Arbroath and working as a flax mill worker.

On their return to Arbroath area after a brief interval, Ann Margaret and John stayed there for the rest of their lives. Ann Margaret died in Arbroath in 1907. The latter part of Ann Margaret's life has been described in conjunction with the life of John Smith in chapter 4.

Chapter 7

Dissidents

The paternal forebears of Agnes Murie Fenwick were dissidents. Initially, the dissidence of the Fenwick line was religious but it was later extended to political disagreement with the established order. The origin of this dissidence was with the established Presbyterian Church of Scotland in the early 1700s but by 1800 it had been widened to the political sphere. Thereafter, both religious and political dissidence were upheld by Agnes's paternal forebears.

The earliest of the Fenwick forbears to appear in records was George, a cottar in Kinclaven, Perthshire, in the late 1600s. George's son, John, senior, was a cottar, who was a member of the Kinclaven congregation that seceded from the Church of Scotland and formed a separate church after 1733. The son of John, senior also named John, was a cottar and part-time weaver in Kinclaven. John's son, Gilbert, became a full-time handloom weaver, moved to Perth in its radical heyday and then during a spell as a soldier, was privy to a mutiny in 1794. Gilbert was the father of Stewart, senior, who abandoned declining handloom weaving for the occupation of warping, in 1850. The son of Stewart senior, also named Stewart, was a leather currier, who left Perth for Aberdeen then moved to Dundee in 1870. Stewart was the father of Agnes, a leather machinist who married James Guthrie Smith in 1906 in Dundee.

Agnes's surname only became standardised in Scotland about 1800. Because spelling was phonetic, there were many variations in the name prior to that date, of which Finnick was one version. Unlike many other surnames, Fenwick does not have occupational origins. Instead, the two sources of the name Fenwick are locative and topographical. The name first appeared in records in Scotland in 1220 in the Borders, in 1313 in Ayrshire and in 1279 in Northumberland, England. Today there are several places named Fenwick, one in Ayrshire, one in Northumberland and one in Yorkshire. The topographical origin of the name is from Anglo-Saxon, where it means dwelling place by a marsh or stream. A form of English was spoken in Lowland Scotland and from that it is inferred that Agnes's early forebears acquired their surname from living near marshy or watery places. The name Fenwick appears in various records for parishes in Perthshire from the late 1600s.

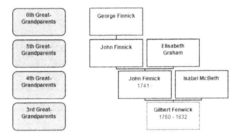

George Fenwick

George Fenwick was the earliest paternal forebear of Agnes to appear in records. His name appeared in the hearth tax record for Kinclaven in 1694. Kinclaven was an ancient parish, seven miles north of Perth, with several small villages in it and with the river Tay running along the boundary of the parish. It was a fertile agricultural area. The hearth tax was a tax liability on each hearth or fireplace in a dwelling and George paid £2 2s 0d for three hearths. Three hearths were apparently the average number for a household in the parish. There was one dwelling with just one hearth. The record shows that George was the sole Fenwick household in the parish. There were one hundred and eighty three hearth tax payers in Kinclaven parish suggesting a population of a few hundred. The poor were exempted from paying the tax. In the parish they numbered four, three of whom were women. With a paucity of historical souces for the time and place, all that can be said with assurance is that George was a peasant or more specifically, a cottar.

John Fenwick, Senior

George's son, John, senior, married Elisabeth Graham in November 1733. John and Elisabeth had eleven children between 1734 and 1755, two of whom died in childhood.

Kinclaven during the 1700s comprised many small arable farms or holdings, between twenty and fifty acres in size. Peasants such as John, senior laboured for the farmers and had small patches of land for their own use. It was common for the peasants in their domestic activities to include weaving linen by males and spinning by females.

John, senior, and Elisabeth Graham, participated in an event of historical significance that became known as the First Secession. The event was a demonstration against the principle of patronage in the Church. It started a movement in Scotland that separated parishes into different camps for decades. It was also an early expression (in the modern period) of political consciousness amongst the common people that gathered pace in following years.

In 1733, the Rev. James Fisher, the minister in Kinclaven, joined three others in protesting at the Church of Scotland's continued acceptance of patronage and he was supported by the whole of the parish. The issue of patronage had been a matter of dispute since the Reformation and particularly since the Patronage Act of 1712. By law, the heritors or landowners in the parish had the right to appoint the minister to a vacancy and thereby exercise considerable control over the whole life of a parish. The four ministers rejected this patronage because it restricted the right of a congregation, through the elders who were elected, to appoint the minister of its choice. All four ministers were suspended so they established a separate Secession Church. The congregation in Kinclaven continued to worship in the church and they were joined by many from neighbouring parishes who withdrew from the Church of Scotland and placed themselves under the Kinclaven minister.

In 1740, the four rebellious ministers were deposed and they and their congregations were ordered to be ejected from their churches by virtue of a Sheriff's warrant. When a new minister was appointed by the Church of Scotland to preach in the vacated church in Kinclaven, he was dragged from his pulpit and thrown outside by angry members of the displaced congregation, mostly women. The seceders or dissenters in Kinclaven worshiped in the open air in summer, as they could not get ground to build a church, and in the winter they met in a barn. This arrangement continued until 1744 when they took possession of a place to worship which they erected for themselves. In due course, the dissenters were able to provide a school for their children. Subsequently, the descendants of John senior in Kinclaven, John and Gilbert, may have been beneficiaries of this provision, if subscriptions were paid for them. A consequence of such schooling was to affirm the identity of pupils as dissenters. In the process of imparting literacy to pupils, a questioning and critical outlook was also engendered.

Patronage became the symbol of the subordination of the Church of Scotland to the upper social orders especially the landed interest. It was perceived as an arrogant extension of secular authority into the Kingdom of Christ. It provoked outrage and exodus from the Church. Accordingly, the example of Kinclaven and the other three parishes attracted widespread support so that by 1745 there were forty-five congregations in the Secession Church. In the late 1700s and in the 1800s, there was more secession from the Church of Scotland over patronage. The seceding churches experienced schisms and also some unification. As a result of secession, the number of dissenting Presbyterians increased hugely. Church patronage was abolished by act of parliament in 1874. All the seceding churches other than a fraction, reunited with the Church of Scotland in 1929.

John Fenwick

John was born in the village of Arntully, Kinclaven, in 1741 and he married Isabel McBeth. The Kinclaven of which John was an inhabitant numbered nine hundred and ninety three in 1755. The communicants of his Secession Church numbered two hundred and forty one, half of them being from neighbouring parishes. Antagonism to the Church of Scotland persisted amongst the dissenters. This was shown in 1754 by a warning being read from the pulpit of the Secession Church against contact with the ministers of the Church of Scotland in the exercise of any parts of their office.

Arntully, the principal village in the parish, consisted of sixty or seventy dwelling houses. It was a peasant village that was ancient in origin, layout and condition and was correspondingly basic in its living conditions, exemplified by there being a midden (for dung, refuse and compost) in front of the entrance to each dwelling. During the 1700s, many of the inhabitants, who had a bit of ground to grow vegetables and to keep a cow, became handloom weavers. This activity was undertaken chiefly during the winter so that the seasonal requirements of agriculture could be met. John had probably acquired the skill of weaving from his father and subsequently passed it onto his son. Initially, handloom weaving of linen was undertaken for the home but over time it came to be undertaken for individual customers rather than for the home only. At first, barter was usually the means of payment but cash became more of a norm in later years as the economy gradually became monetised in rural areas. If the material spun by a weaver's wife provided an insufficient supply for an increasing number of customers, it was usual for the weaver to collect the raw material from spinners in the neighbourhood.

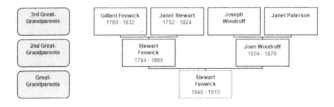

Gilbert Fenwick

Gilbert was born in 1760 in Kinclaven According to the church registers, he had no siblings. If he was an only child then his family was unusually small for the time. It is more probable that the births of Gilbert's siblings were not registered because his parents upheld dissenter customs. Registration of births was reduced by the refusal of dissenters to inform ministers of the Church of Scotland because they feared a corrupting influence from contact with them.

Gilbert grew up in Kinclaven in the late 1700s where handloom weaving was widespread amongst the local population. However, changes were occurring whereby it was no longer the norm for weaving to be done for the home and individual customers. Instead, it was increasingly common for the handloom weavers to be engaged in the 'putting out' system. The weavers were employed by manufacturers or their agents in Perth who supplied them with the raw material to be woven into coarse linen cloth. Linen manufacture in Perth expanded during Gilbert's early years so that he may have been given enough orders to make a good living wholly as a weaver, instead of a cottar who did weaving as subsidiary activity.

By 1788 Gilbert had left Kinclaven to live in Perth. The linen that was woven in Kinclaven was transported to Perth by the weavers using horses and carts. Perth was only a few miles away and Gilbert's introduction to the town may have been from transporting woven linen or marketing agricultural produce there. He could have recognised that Perth offered him a better living as a full-time handloom weaver than Kinclaven. It had already established itself as a major textile centre with seventy three spinning mills for linen in 1772. However, in moving from rural Kinclaven to urban Perth, Gilbert was putting all his eggs into one basket. For Perth, could not offer a handloom weaver casual employment in agriculture as a backup for hard times.

In 1778 in Perth, Gilbert married Janet Stewart. Between 1788 and 1796, four children were born to them. Janet Stewart's upbringing was in the Church of Scotland for she was from Fortingall parish, Perthshire, where there was no dissenting church. Gilbert and Janet resolved whatever religious differences they had by accepting that both their churches had a place in their lives. They married in the Church of Scotland but the two eldest children were baptised in the dissenting Perth Relief Church. The Relief Church claimed to provide relief for congregations oppressed by the patronage system. The two youngest children were baptised in the Church of Scotland when Gilbert was absent from home on military service. The births of all four children were registered with the Church of Scotland.

When Gilbert moved to Perth, the town was a growing place with a variety of industries in which textiles were of primary importance. The population was nine thousand and nineteen in 1755 and fourteen thousand, eight hundred and seventy eight in 1801. In the 1790s, handloom weavers numbered fifteen hundred, therefore a significant occupational group in the town's population. The handloom weavers were employed not only by manufacturers in Perth but by agents on behalf of manufacturers in other towns such as Glasgow and Paisley. Cotton was introduced into the town for spinning and weaving at around 1787 and after 1810, it superseded linen as the staple textile although both co-existed in the town for many years. As a handloom weaver, Gilbert worked at home with materials that were brought to him. The handloom weavers had looms either in workshops or in sheds that adjoined their homes. Handloom weavers were effectively piece workers who were paid on satisfactory completion of work. Generally, (there were variations) the weavers enjoyed good wages and living conditions. They were a community proud of their skill, conscious of their superior status above common labourers and the most numerous category of artisan in Scotland in the late 1700s.

As an inhabitant of Perth, Gilbert lived at a time of great political turbulence which enveloped his town as much as any in Scotland, and perhaps more so. Only the big property owners could vote, 0.2% of the population of Scotland, and there was a growing popular feeling that the political system was archaic, corrupt and moribund. The French Revolution had occurred in 1789 and had stimulated debate over the ideas associated with it. In different quarters, the event prompted fear and opposition and hope and support. Ideas for political reform were stirred up which were further encouraged by the publication of *The Rights of Man* by Thomas Paine. Part One was published in 1791 and Part Two published in 1792. Paine's text defended liberty, equality and brotherhood - the values of the Revolution and supported republicanism and democratic government. It proposed a welfare state. Thomas Paine was decades ahead of his time. Ideas for political reform were promoted by the formation of societies throughout Scotland and in Perth, a society was formed called the Revolution Club. In 1790 a certificate of membership listed these Perth radicals by forename and surname but eleven were identified by surname only. Of these eleven, one was a Fenwick. Perhaps it was Gilbert.

In July 1792, Friends of the People branches were formed all over the central belt in Scotland. The Friends of the People campaigned for democratic change seeking adult suffrage and annual parliaments. This was a broad movement for political change which included radicals of different hues, some moderate in their demands, others with a wider and deeper commitment to radical change. In August 1792, a Friends of the People Society was formed in Perth and by October there were nine Friends of the People branches in the town with a membership of twelve hundred. The Society sent nine delegates to the first Scottish Convention in Edinburgh in December. Member of Friends of the People in Perth included three dissenting ministers, of whom one was Rev. David Sangster, the minister of the United Relief Church. Rev. David Sangster had baptised the two eldest children of Gilbert in 1788 and 1790 and he was listed as a member of the Revolution Club of Perth in 1790. His sermons addressed current issues that were of concern which included political matters. The Perth United Relief Church had opened in 1786 with eleven of the fourteen names on its title deeds being handloom weavers. Its building was used as a meeting place by Friends of the People. In 1794, Rev. David Sangster was denounced by four members of his congregation for preaching in support of the French revolution and against the war with France.

In Perth, in November 1792, there were disturbances when a Tree of Liberty was erected in the town and an effigy of Henry Dundas, the Home Secretary and political overlord of Scotland, was hung and set on fire. Huge meetings were held in the town. The Duke of Atholl, caught up in the demonstrations was forced to shout for liberty and equality. Friends of the People dissociated themselves from the riots at which support was voiced for Liberty Equality and no King. The Commander of the Army in Scotland, Lord Adam Gordon described Perth as a 'very dangerous place' and the government became so alarmed they sent troops into the town where republican slogans were displayed. A barracks was erected in the town in 1795. The government used spies to keep informed about what the radicals were doing and the formation of loyalist groups was stimulated and efforts were made to discredit and vilify radicals. Even with the distortion of information by the authorities, there was evidence that some radicals in Perth (and elsewhere in Scotland) were looking to armed revolution. Overall, Perth appears to have been a place that simmered politically between 1789 and 1815 and was not governed easily during this time.

Gilbert's residence in Perth, his occupation as a handloom weaver and his religious beliefs as a dissenter strongly suggest that he supported radical political change throughout his life.

The handloom weavers were in the vanguard of those supporting political change. They stood apart from fellow workers in terms of both literacy and general education. They were avid readers of radical newspapers and pamphlets and some were familiar with the theory of Thomas Paine. Their families sustained a lively culture of political debate and discussion. Compared to their numbers in the working class, there was a disproportionate contribution by handloom weavers to bodies advocating radical change. Friends of the People societies were formed in weaving towns and handloom weavers were their principal supporters. A successor to the Friends of the People societies (which collapsed as a result of government repression) was the secret and plebian United Scotsmen, many of whose members were handloom weavers. In trials for sedition that were brought against radicals during the war with France, most of those accused and their witnesses were handloom weavers.

The dissenters like the weavers, (and there were many who were both) were also frequently to be found amongst those in support of radical political change. Of the population of Perth in the 1790s, a third was in the dissenting churches. Dissenting ministers were occasionally responsible for spreading radical doctrines but they did not support violence. Dissenters had broken with the Church of Scotland to reject patronage and they were inclined to arrive at the same view when they considered the government of the country. The ministers of the Relief Church in particular, did not lose their enthusiasm for the French revolution. In the later 1700s, ministers contributed to the emergence of political awareness amongst the common people. They encouraged literacy to read and interrogate the bible which opened up a questioning attitude that extended beyond religion. Independence of thought emerged amongst the dissenters from which many were drawn to democratic politics.

In contrast to the dissenting churches, the ministers of the Church of Scotland in general, made vigorous efforts to quell radical thinking. This was exemplified by the Perth Minister, who in his contribution to the *Old Statistical Account* opined that Thomas Paine was visionary and irreligious and his book was part of a dangerous tendency.

The radical political activity that surfaced in Perth and Scotland in 1792 was followed by a decline in the subsequent year. Fear of invasion and repression by the government changed the political climate. A number of radicals were arrested, tried and sentenced to imprisonment for sedition.

The suppression of radicalism in 1793 was accompanied by economic austerity. There was an economic depression with an ensuing decline in levels of employment. In February 1793, France declared war on Britain and it adversely affected the export of textiles which impacted on wages and employment. The depression of 1793 meant that thousands went on poor relief, emigrated or joined the army, just to survive. Gilbert was one of the latter, his response to the dire economic circumstances which faced him. For him, the impact of the depression could have been aggravated by his support for radicalism. For those who were overtly radical, were suspected of treachery and found that manufacturers eschewed putting work to them. Gilbert was not alone in his economic adversity. The harshness of the times had its effect on the Friends of the People. The meeting of its Convention in October 1793 was poorly attended (there was only one delegate from Perth), because the branches which had become largely working class in their membership, were unable to afford to pay for delegates to travel to the Convention in Edinburgh.

In 1793, Gilbert enlisted into the Breadalbane Fencibles, whose headquarters were in Perth. It was an infantry regiment, one of seven that the War Office ordered for Scotland in March 1793 in response to the declaration of war by France. The term 'fencible' probably comes from 'defencible' and means a defence force. These Scottish regiments were formed by the leading Clan Chiefs and landowners. The fourth Earl of Breadalbane, Sir John Campbell, recruited two battalions initially for service in Scotland only. A third battalion was raised in 1794 for service in Ireland and many of its recruits were volunteers from the first two battalions. The number recruited by the Earl of Breadalbane was two thousand and three hundred although the number was reduced after two years. Sixteen hundred were recruited from the Breadalbane estate that stretched across Perthshire and Argyll. The remainder was recruited from the rest of the county of Perthshire. Thus the core of the regiment was from the Highlands, mainly tenants, cottars and crofters, the minority being Lowlanders of whom Gilbert was one. Although the Highlanders differed from Gilbert in being Gaelic speaking clansman, they were similar to him in motivation for enlistment. For both, their military service was a matter of economic expediency. Economic necessity had prompted Gilbert's enlistment and from their enlistment the Highlanders expected promises to be fulfilled to improve their families' tenuous claims to land.

The three battalions of the regiment were organised into several companies, and Gilbert's company was under the command of Captain Alexander Campbell and in the first battalion. It had a lieutenant, an ensign, three sergeants, three corporals, two drummers and forty seven privates. The Breadalbane Fencibles had two pipers for each of its battalions and its uniform was highland dress in the form of belted plaid (a full length garment that could be worn as a cloak) on duty and a kilt (the bottom half of the belted plaid) off duty.

For Gilbert, the benefits of service in the Breadalbanes were several. He was paid a bounty of three guineas on enlistment and thereafter, a shilling for each of the seven days in a week. He now had pay that could help to support his family. He was clothed and fed (including four and half pounds of oatmeal every four days), and could expect medical attention, if required. Because his military service was restricted to Scotland and exceptionally England, injury or death was only a serious risk should there be an invasion by the French. In 1791 the average wage in Perth for a handloom weaver was 15s 4d per fortnight. Therefore Gilbert's enlistment secured an income that was as good as or better than his earnings prior to the economic downturn of 1793.

Two events throw some light on the attitude of Gilbert and his comrades in arms. The men recruited to the first and second battalions made it clear that they were unwilling to serve other than in Scotland which required the Earl of Breadalbane to raise a third battalion for service elsewhere. Furthermore, soon after formation when a battalion of the fencibles was ordered to leave Perth and march to Kinross, the men did not move. They were unwilling to do so until they were paid arrears of pay. They only did so when given assurance about the payment of the arrears. Therefore it seems that that the men had been influenced by Thomas Paine's *Rights of Man* and their attitude had changed as a result. They had acquired knowledge of what was their due and also the courage to demand it.

This sense of entitlement of the enlisted men undoubtedly contributed to the mutiny that occurred in the first battalion, after the regiment was moved to Glasgow in July 1794. In this event, Gilbert's exact experience can only be imagined. In November 1794, a private on guard duty, who was escorting a prisoner, a deserter from another regiment, by chance, failed to stop him escaping. As a result, the private, Hugh Robertson, a man of good character, was confined and faced a court martial with the prospect of a minimum of three hundred lashes. The men of Hugh Robertson's company and others used muskets and fixed bayonets to force his release. They had already been required to watch one man being punished by a public flogging in July and they were unwilling to let it happen again. They also had some other grievances. The Glasgow population with whom the men had been quartered, rioted and showed their support.

There appears to have been extensive support for the mutiny throughout the one thousand- strong first battalion. Certainly, the Commander in Chief of the Army in Scotland seemed to think that disaffection was widespread in the first battalion for he ordered troops to surround Glasgow. They were to subdue the mutiny if necessary but first the mutineers were given time to restore military discipline themselves. After a fortnight in which the men paraded as expected each day, they abandoned their mutiny in December and surrendered Hugh Robertson to custody together with a few who volunteered to stand trial as ringleaders on behalf of all the mutineers. The first battalion was moved to Edinburgh where court martials took place. Six men were in effect, exiled, by compulsory service in another regiment overseas. Three of them were also given five hundred strokes of the lash each. Hugh Sutherland was executed on Musselburgh sands by a firing party of twelve from his regiment on 27 January 1795. The mutiny in the first battalion highlights the savage military discipline that Gilbert was subject to and the solidarity and courage of the men of the first battalion who challenged it, albeit to their detriment.

After 1795, Gilbert's battalion was stationed at different places around Scotland that included Lithlingow, Falkirk, Ayr, Stranraer, Aberden, Elgin and Fort George.

The first and second battalions of the Breadalbane Fencibles were disbanded in 1799 because militia regiments had now been formed in Scotland in their stead. The third battalion remained on service in Ireland. On disbandment, a third of the men of the Breadalbane Fencibles joined the regular army for service in Ireland but Gilbert was not amongst them. His enlistment as a fencible was to replace his loss of earnings as a handloom weaver when the textile industry slumped. He had not been persuaded that military service offered him a life that was preferable to being a handloom weaver. Instead, it had perhaps left him with a memory of an unjust, barbarous, punishment, and a confirmation of his belief in the necessity of radical political change from below, to create a fairer society.

On discharge from the Fencibles, Gilbert returned to the handloom weaver community in Perth. The handloom weaver community was also a part of the life of Gilbert's son Stewart, senior and it is described later in this chapter. In 1802 Gilbert was living in South Street where many in his trade lived. A militia census of the population that year listed him as liable for service but his previous military experience enabled him to obtain exemption from conscription. More than three hundred and fifty three of the town's weavers were listed for service in the militia by the census.

Although Gilbert's experience of a slump forced him to abandon handloom weaving for soldiering for a time, the evidence overall suggests that there was a 'golden age' for his occupation in Scotland between 1790 and 1810. During this period handloom weavers continued to enjoy high wages and good living standards compared to others. To defend their high wages and good living conditions weavers organised themselves into unions. In 1809 a General Association of Operative Weavers was formed in Scotland. A central committee was formed that included representatives from the local committee in Perth. In 1812 to secure better wages, a nationwide strike of handloom weavers occurred in Scotland that involved forty thousand workers and lasted nine weeks. The weavers were defeated and the union broken with its leaders being imprisoned.

In the remaining years of Gilbert's life, the handloom weavers experienced hardship from the start of a decline in their occupation as a result of several factors. One important factor was a swelling in numbers in the occupation and a fall in wages and living standards. The decline of the occupation continued during the life of Gilbert's son Stewart, senior, also in the same occupation. Gilbert's wife Janet Stewart died in 1824 and he died in 1832. Both were buried in the town's Greyfriars cemetery. Of their four children, it may have been Stewart senior, who looked after them in their later years.

His support of his parents might account for him marrying at the relatively late age of forty four, after their deaths.

Stewart Fenwick, Senior

Stewart, senior, the younger son of Gilbert and Janet was born into the Perth handloom weaver community in 1794 and accordingly, learned the craft of his father. As the workplace of the handloom weaver was his home, all the family could help in some way with the process. If Stewart received education it was in one of the dissenters' schools in the town. In the early years of Stewart, senior, good wages were paid to handloom weavers but after 1815, there was a real fall in their value. Moreover, handloom weaving was subject to cyclical slumps (as it had been for Gilbert) and so Stewart, senior, experienced fluctuations in work, wages and living standards, with bouts of unemployment and poverty. During this period, the weavers of Perth protested at their plight through demonstrations and big meetings that were held on South Inch.

The working experience of handloom weavers worsened further after 1830. Official enquiries suggested that in 1834 half of Scotland's handloom weavers were living in poverty and for protracted periods. The Scottish textile industry stagnated after 1830. It was beset by competition from Lancashire and abroad. Profit margins were small and there was intense competition between small manufacturers. There was an over-supply of labour so wages could be cut. The gradual introduction of the powerloom, (later in Scotland than in England), also made its impact on handloom weaving. It offered manufacturers greater productivity and permitted the employment of workers with much lesser skill. Changes occurred in the ways of working of handloom weavers so that they were less able to control the manner and pace of their work. They increasingly spent longer hours at their looms to offset cutbacks in living standards as piece rates fell. The hours that Stewart, senior, worked in the 1830s were probably seventy to eighty hours a week starting at 6.00 am.

As a handloom weaver, Stewart, senior, gradually lost the status of an independent artisan. In Perth, the fall in work for handloom weavers reduced their numbers in the town from three thousand in 1810 to eighteen hundred in 1836. In 1836 as a result of a public meeting in Perth chaired by the Lord Provost, a distress fund was started to relieve the distress of the weavers. The local Member of Parliament sent ten pounds to the relief fund in 1840.

From their residential concentration, the handloom weavers had a strong sense of community. Although they typically worked on their own, they required help for some processes such as setting up the warp. They assisted one another with this task which often took place in the evening so as not to impinge on weaving time. On these occasions the weavers socialised and food and drink were supplied. They also enjoyed a rich cultural life buying books and composing poetry and songs. In Perth, the handloom weavers formed a Pomarium flute band that participated in political demonstrations in the town, for example over the proposed Reform Bills of 1832 and 1867. The handloom weavers shared the same fate and fortunes and they developed mutual assistance through the formation of friendly societies.

A Perth Operative Weavers Friendly Society was instituted at Perth in November 1805. It gave financial assistance during the hard times of sickness, infirmity, death, unemployment and serious accidents from the subscriptions of members and from fines. There were quarterly meetings for members who had to be of good character. Fines were imposed on members for drunkenness, street wrangling, disorderly conduct and swearing. Members were expelled from the Society for serious criminal offences. The records of the Society in Perth have not survived but historical evidence about friendly societies in Scotland suggests their activities. The societies bought foodstuffs and other household requirements in bulk at times when goods were cheap and sold them a little under market price to their members, giving credit if requested. The societies' funds were sometimes used to buy books and even establish libraries. The societies also afforded a space to debate and discuss matters of concern. Some societies operated a form of credit union, where people could borrow money from the communal funds at a fixed rate of interest. The dissenting churches also collected money from their congregations which they dispensed to poor members. These arrangements were independent of the poor law administered by the Church of Scotland until 1845. Little help could be expected from the poor law for handloom weavers.

In 1839, in the Perth United Associate Church, Stewart, senior, married Joan Woodroff, who was ten years younger and a widowed mother. She had been brought up by her mother from infancy after her father, a sergeant in the army, had died in 1806, on military service abroad during the Napoleonic war. Her two Perth- born children from her first marriage became the step-children of Stewart, senior. Joan had married William Paton, a Perth-born plasterer in 1831 and they had moved from Edinburgh to Perth, where he had died of tuberculosis in 1838. Between 1840 and 1851 Stewart senior and Joan had six children, one of whom died in childhood. In keeping with dissenter custom, the births of their children were not registered with the Church of Scotland, with the exception of the eldest child, Stewart. He was baptised by an elder of the Glasite Church which suggests that Joan was a member. It was a dissenting church founded in 1730 by John Glas, a minister who was deposed from the Church of Scotland because of his beliefs in primitive Christianity and the autonomy of the local congregation. The church had no ministers, leadership was by elders and it held that the accumulation of wealth was unscriptural and improper. It remained a very small sect that never unified with others and has not survived, although its church buildings have, one is in Perth.

In 1842, Stewart, senior, and Joan lived in Pomarium, one of the ninety five handloom weaver households in the street. Although the handloom weavers lived all around the town, Pomarium, High Street and Leonard Street had concentrations of them. The railway came to Perth in 1848 with the line to Dundee passing at the end of their street. There was a railway terminus and goods shed nearby and the railway goods manager became a proprietor of houses in Pomarium that included the house of Stewart, senior, and Joan. The decline in handloom weavers was shown by the increase of other occupations amongst the tenants. In 1855, the neighbours of Stewart senior and Joan included labourers, a grain dealer, a plasterer, a mason, a slater, an engine driver, a railway porter, a refuse collector and a policeman.

Perth still had radical political activity for Stewart, senior, to support whilst he lived there. There was a Perth Chartist Association which organised meetings attended by several hundred people between 1839 and 1842. Its chair was John Cree, a handloom weaver. Besides Chartism, Stewart, senior, may have engaged in weaver union activities also.

The mechanisation of weaving in Perth proceeded throughout the life of Stewart, senior, and handlooms seriously contracted after 1840. In his later years it became increasingly difficult for Stewart, senior, to earn a sufficient wage from his traditional occupation. He found work was available as a warper, another textile occupation in Perth, and so he moved back and forth between warping in the weaving factory and weaving at the handloom attached to his home. A warper arranged the individual yarns which created the "warp" of the fabric upon a large cylinder called a beam, prior to the yarn being woven. By 1850, Stewart had abandoned handloom weaving to become a warper full-time, for the rest of his life. The small number of handlooms still in use was largely for fine and fancy specialists. It seems that Stewart eschewed becoming a powerloom weaver because the earnings of a warper were better. The difference in pay is illustrated by textile operatives in the nearby Dundee jute industry in 1853. The average pay for a sixty hour week for a warper was between twelve and sixteen shillings whereas a powerloom weaver was paid eight to eleven shillings per week. Powerloom weaving was increasingly the job of women with lesser earnings. In becoming a warper, Stewart senior lost the dwindling independence from being a handloom weaver in return for a more stable and predictable income, accompanied by a shorter working week.

In the Fenwick household, Stewart, senior, was not alone as a textile operative. His wife, Joan and his step-daughter, Joan, were also employed in the textile industry as winders. Their job was to wind the thread onto weaving looms. Stewart, senior, and Joan remained in the declining weaver community of Pomarium until their deaths at the respective ages of seventy, in 1865 and seventy two, in 1878.

Stewart Fenwick

Stewart Fenwick was born in 1840 in Perth. Any formal education that he received was most probably in a dissenters' school in the town. In his early childhood, Stewart may have learned some aspects of the craft of handloom weaving from his father, using the loom at home. However, any expectations that he or his father had of him following this occupation became unrealistic. The textile industry was still a large employer in Perth in Stewart's early years but Stewart eschewed employment in the industry to become a currier. Leather manufacture had been an important industry in Perth historically but had declined considerably by the time Stewart was an apprentice. He followed the example of his elder step-brother, William, when he became a currier. It offered him a skilled trade with a commensurate reward that was greater than unskilled labouring in its various forms. The currier was employed by leather merchants in villages, towns and cities throughout Scotland because the industry was dispersed. It was necessary to serve an apprenticeship to enter the occupation and that started between the ages of twelve to fourteen and lasted seven years.

The curriers were a separate occupation from the tanners at this time and so tanneries were separate establishments. That is not so today. Curriers usually worked in workshops that were smaller than tanneries. Typically, an establishment employed twenty five to thirty curriers whereas a tannery might employ up to one hundred and fifty workers. In rural areas, currying and tanning were more of a cottage industry and so the number of employees in a business in a town the size of Perth was probably very small. The currying workshops could be tiny and primitive in their conditions.

In becoming a currier, Stewart's job began when the tanning was completed. The tanning process subjected the animal hides or skins to immersion in chemicals to clean, preserve and remove hair and fat. The process of currying involved stretching the tanned leather on a variety of different frames and finishing it to make it supple and strong for the use of a saddler or cobbler. The currier pared or shaved the leather to a level of uniform thickness, then dyed or coloured it by treating it with oils or greases and then treating the grainy surface with a wax dubbing or shellac finish. The hides were dressed so they became smooth and waterproof. The work was done all by hand and was very laborious. Currying was hard manual labour that needed strength, skill and the use of specialist hand tools. There was no mechanisation of the process at this time.

Curriers were usually paid by the hour. In 1869 the average wage for curriers was twenty six shillings a week in Scotland. In the same year, there were three thousand curriers in Britain, of whom only three hundred were in Scotland. Their usual working week was fifty five hours. About half of the curriers were trade unionists. Stewart may have experienced some fluctuation in his wages as demand for leather goods fluctuated but it was not akin to the huge cyclical variation that handloom weaving experienced. Stewart became an artisan like his father. But unlike his father, his occupation was more stable and did not become obsolete because of technological change.

Stewart left Perth on completion of his apprenticeship about 1862 and as a journeyman he moved to Aberdeen to work. In 1861, Perth's population was only thirty five thousand, with four businesses at most, that employed curriers. By employing apprentices rather than journeymen, an employer could reduce his wage bill. Accordingly, there may have been no vacancies for journeymen curriers when Stewart completed his apprenticeship. In which case, he had to spread his wings and move to a place that offered him work. Aberdeen was twice the size of Perth, with a population of seventy four thousand in 1861. There were nine employers of curriers in 1862, twice the number that were in business in Perth. In addition to its employment opportunities, Aberdeen offered to a young single man the attraction of big city life. However, the employers of curriers in Aberdeen had dwindled to four by 1870. The decline in employment may have hit Stewart personally, making it a necessity to move again to find work.

Before he moved, Stewart met and courted Agnes Pearson. They lived in separate lodgings in the same street and she worked as a seamstress. Agnes's family originated from Perth and so she may have first made his acquaintance there. They married in Aberdeen in 1869, in the United Presbyterian Church. Stewart's loyalty to dissent took precedence over Agnes's Church of Scotland upbringing. They left Aberdeen for Dundee in 1870.

Dundee offered good employment prospects for Stewart. Dundee in 1871 was a city with a population of one hundred and twenty thousand, where leather and boot and shoe making had long been important industries. There were eight employers of curriers. Stewart and Agnes left Dundee between 1876 and 1879 for Perth, where he continued in his trade as a currier with one of the four employers in his trade. This move suggests that there was no work for Stewart in his trade in Dundee, although unskilled work may have been available to him. Wishing to maintain the pay of a skilled man, he returned to his birthplace. In Perth, Stewart was able to maintain closer contact with his mother and his siblings. His mother died in 1878. Stewart and Agnes moved back to Dundee which suggests that work for him had finished in Perth and he found that his trade had revived in the bigger city.

Soon after his return to Dundee, in January 1880, Stewart had the sad experience of having to identify the body of his younger, single, brother, Gilbert, a journeyman dyer, who had drowned in the river Tay. Gilbert, was on a visit to Dundee from Perth and despondent over finding no work, had committed suicide. Stewart's siblings Joseph, and Helen, died respectively in 1872 and 1888 from tuberculosis. Tuberculosis was one of the biggest killers, particularly of younger people in Scotland, until 1950. It was closely associated with poverty and urban squalor.

In Dundee, between 1870 and 1883, seven children were born to Stewart and Agnes, one of whom died in infancy. The city's leather industry was sufficiently buoyant for Stewart to remain in employment as a currier for the remainder of his working life. In 1906, there were thirteen employers of curriers in the city. Stewart and Agnes had several addresses in Dundee during their time there. Their moves were probably to obtain more rooms as their family grew and also to get rents they could afford. The annual rental value of their tenancy in 1875 was £9 12s compared to £14 0s in 1905. In Dundee, Agnes maintained contact with her siblings. Her single younger sister, Allison became a lodger for a time. Visits also were made by Margaret, a married sister of Agnes who lived in Inverness.

In 1901 all the children of Stewart and Agnes were still living in the parental home. Thirty one year old Stewart was a commercial traveller, twenty nine year old Joseph was a jute mill mechanic, twenty seven year old James was a stone mason, twenty four year old Elizabeth was a mother's help, twenty year old Agnes was a leather machinist and seventeen year old George was a clerk.

In their last years Stewart and Agnes lived with their daughter Agnes and her husband.

Agnes Murie Fenwick

Agnes was born in Dundee in 1881 and left school at the age of thirteen in 1894. Her schooling was different from her forebears because the education system after 1872 was under the control of the State rather than the churches. Whilst she was not formally educated as a dissenter, her upbringing was in a home where the tradition of dissent was upheld. From her father, she was exposed to a questioning and critical disposition towards the established social order.

For females in Dundee at this time, the jute industry was a large employer but Agnes opted for shoe making and became a leather machinist. Her employment suggests the influence of her currier father and seamstress mother. As a machinist, she made holes in the parts of the shoe which she stitched together. The process for which she was employed was called closing and it followed on from the work of the clicker. Seams were stitched with silk, cotton or linen. Sewing machines were mainly used for the task. The task of closing required great skill as stitch formation was as important as the clicking process. The stitch tension was vital as each stitch had to be bed down to the upper and be in keeping with the style of the shoe.

Agnes became a member of the National Union of Boot and Shoe Operatives. Although this trade union enjoyed a substantial female membership after 1911, at the time Agnes was a member, female membership was small. In fact, before 1911, about ninety per cent of all trade unionists were men and over ninety per cent of women workers were unorganised. Agnes was one of a small number of women whose values and beliefs were expressed by trade unions. In her case, her family background predisposed her to challenge the prevailing order rather than to acquiesce to it.

In Dundee, Agnes met James Guthrie Smith, a shoe clicker, and they were married in the Church of Scotland in 1906. Differences between the Church of Scotland and the dissenting churches had lessened greatly by this time. James was a trade unionist and socialist and Agnes shared his political outlook. Two of Agnes's brothers also upheld the family's political tradition through their support for a stronger version of socialist politics than James Smith espoused. Agnes's life after her marriage to James Guthrie Smith is described in chapter 5.

Chapter 8

Stitchers

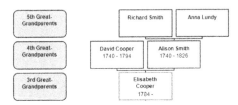

The maternal forebears of Agnes Fenwick were stitchers. Amongst the common people, sewing was just one of the regular domestic activities performed by women. Women not only made clothing they extended the longevity of items of clothing. Sewing was used for mending. Clothing that was faded would be turned inside-out so that it could continue to be worn, and sometimes had to be taken apart and reassembled in order to suit this purpose. In the 1800s, needlework came to be an activity that was widely undertaken beyond the household for payment.

Agnes Fenwick's maternal forebears originated from the county of Fife in east Scotland and the earliest in order of descent were, Anna Lundy, Alison Smith and Elisabeth Cooper. It was Elisabeth Cooper who extended the domestic chore of sewing to an activity that was a supplementary means for earning cash. Subsequently, for Agnes Murie, Agnes Pearson and Agnes Murie Fenwick, sewing became the means by which they earned a living. The description of these forebears as stitchers identifies one important aspect of their lives that they shared. However, their lives were about much more than sewing, as the chapter will show.

Anna Lundy

The earliest recorded forebear of Agnes Fenwick was Anna Lundy. Between 1738 and 1740, she and Richard Smith became the parents of two children in the parish of Scoonie, Fife. Nine miles from Kirkcaldy, Scoonie was populated by one thousand, five hundred and twenty eight people in 1755. The majority of the inhabitants lived in Leven, the sole village in the parish. Scoonie was a coastal parish on the north bank of the Firth of Forth. There was a harbour and the parish's few vessels engaged in trade. There was also a seam of coal that had been mined from the late 1600s. Whilst such crops as wheat, barley and oats were grown in the parish, a principal economic activity was the weaving of linen. The parish had its own bleachfield. At this time, in rural parishes like Scoonie, peasant households generated cash income through domestic industry. Eighty per cent of adult women were involved in spinning in Scotland in the 1700s. It is likely therefore, that Anna, like her female peers, was busy spinning flax, in addition to other activities.

Alison Smith

Alison Smith was born in 1740 in Scoonie, Fife. Most probably, Alison learned from her mother how to spin flax amongst other skills. For young single females, domestic or farm service was the norm. Alison married David Cooper, a stonemason, in Scoonie in 1765. They had three daughters between 1766 and 1784. Interestingly, Scoonie had no local quarry. As a stonemason, David was liable to travel to get work and by 1784 he and Alison had moved to Strathmiglo, fourteen miles from Scoonie. Strathmiglo was well supplied with local stone used for building purposes. But the parish did not detain him for long for he and Alison soon moved another fourteen miles to Perth, a growing town. The work in Perth and district for stonemasons was perhaps more plentiful. In the 1700s, women were involved in a wide range of tasks in the household that included cooking, cleaning, child minding and the making and mending of clothes. Skill with the needle was essential for the latter two activities. Alison had probably acquired that skill, amongst others from her mother. Both David and Alison lived in Perth until their respective deaths in 1794 and 1826,

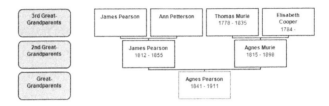

Elisabeth Cooper

Elisabeth Cooper was born in Strathmiglo, Fife, in 1784. Her early years were in Strathmiglo and then Perth. Given that Perth was mainly a textile town, it is most likely that she was employed initially in the manufacture of linen or cotton.

Elisabeth's life was changed by her marriage in 1803, to Thomas Murie, a native of Perth. On their marriage, he was a sergeant in the Royal Perthshire Militia and so subsequently, this military institution exercised much influence on her married life. This influence was considerable and was symbolised early on by the permission to marry that a militiaman was expected to obtain from his commanding officer.

Thomas Murie joined the militia at the age of twenty, on its re-introduction to Scotland in 1798, as a result of the threat that France presented to Britain. On enlistment, he had prior military experience from being a member of the Royal Perth Volunteers for well over a year. From being a Volunteer, he had enlisted in the militia as a substitute for a conscript, who could afford to escape conscription by paying for another to substitute for him. Many militiamen were like Thomas in being substitutes. The motivation for volunteering in the militia was a desire for travel and adventure, wearing a smart uniform, as well as dissatisfaction with a civilian occupation.

Thomas was a glover's son, who like his father, worked in leather but as a shoemaker. His craft required serving an apprenticeship and was not a lucrative occupation. Leather manufacture was second in importance as an industry to textiles in Perth in 1798. From being in the Volunteers, Thomas found that military life suited him and the militia confirmed that so he opted for it instead of shoemaking. Within a fortnight of his enlistment, in the militia, he was promoted to corporal and a few months later he was promoted to sergeant. Several years later, Thomas became a sergeant-major, the rank he retained for the rest of his service. Progress to becoming a commissioned officer was closed to him because it was dependent upon the ownership of property.

Thomas kept a diary of his militia service between 1798 and 1801 and a seventeen page transcript of it was made by a great-granddaughter (Janet McLellan) in 1950. The transcript is now deposited in Perth and Kinross Archives where it is a valuable primary source that is consulted by scholars of the period. As a result, Thomas has become a minor historical celebrity.

From his diary, it is evident that for three years Thomas's regiment was stationed either in barracks or billeted with the inhabitants of towns outside Perthshire, such as Ayr, Greenock, Kilmarnock, Stonehaven and Stirling. Thomas described in detail the many places in Scotland that he visited and it is apparent that he enjoyed being an explorer of his own country. Besides being drilled, marching between towns and participating in reviews by senior officers, Thomas's experience included escorting deserters to embarkation ports for Ireland and recruitment and guard duty. Guard duty in Glasgow necessitated reinforcement during the night because of disturbances over the high price of food. Thomas was very impressed by Glasgow's elegant layout, buildings, facilities and bustle. Glasgow was also the place where he fell ill from 'bloody flux' – dysentery. Military accommodation was often overcrowded and insanitary so communicable diseases flourished. Thomas was complimentary about the barracks which accommodated one thousand and eight men but he was silent about the latrines, if any, their ratio to men, and their condition. He did notice that the separate barracks for officers had privies. Ill for a fortnight, Thomas was hospitalised and recovered. Not all those afflicted as he was, did so. Thomas's diary also illuminated the exercise of military discipline. An anonymous written complaint about conditions made to the Commander in Chief, was followed by another made to the Regiment's Commanding Officer. The anonymous author of both complaints was identified, court martialled and given five hundred lashes. The militia was no different to the rest of the British army when it came to discipline.

Thomas's life as a non-commissioned officer in the militia differed from the privates who were part-time soldiers. As a non-commissioned officer, he was a full-time soldier, a permanent member of staff with regular pay and a pension on discharge. However, his wife, Elisabeth had to contend with his regiment being stationed away from Perth for varying periods. The wives of military personnel faced the challenge of frequent and long periods of separation. These periods could antagonise them from the control that the Military exercised over their lives but also conferred a sense of belonging and pride.

Between 1798 and 1815 the Royal Perthshire Militia was stationed in Glasgow, Fort George, Aberdeen, Banff, Perth, Dunbar, Haddington, Ramsgate, Ashford, Canterbury, Dover, Edinburgh, Penicuick, Carlisle, Shrewsbury, Exeter, Dartmouth, Plymouth and Newcastle. Travel to and from these destinations was mainly on foot, marching, but sometimes by boat. Had Thomas kept a diary of his military life after 1801, his observations would have been very interesting.

Between 1804 and 1825, whilst Thomas was stationed elsewhere, Elisabeth gave birth to nine children in Perth, three of whom died in infancy. Children were costly and Elisabeth was successful in her application for the dependents allowances paid by the militia. Records confirm that she received these for herself and for the three eldest children. This was a weekly payment of one shilling and sixpence for each dependent which undoubtedly helped with the costs of raising the children. The granting of the allowances also confirmed the family's straitened circumstances. Elisabeth had to attest that she was in poverty, had children less than ten years of age, was unable to maintain herself and had no other means than Thomas's pay.

Some militia wives accompanied their husbands on their postings away from home and it is possible that Elisabeth did so for some of the time that Thomas's regiment was stationed away. Wives required a senior officer's permission to accompany their husbands and they were expected to carry their weight. They became subject to the rules and regulations of the militia. Military documents referred to them as 'on the strength'. They might live in the garrison or outside it. It was common for wives to perform various domestic chores for which they were paid. They performed vital services in support of the militia that allowed it to function. The work that a militia wife did was often as a cook, a nurse, a laundress, or a seamstress. The tasks were performed for the small unit to which their husbands belonged. Although clothing was generally made by contractors and altered by militia tailors when regiments received it, militia wives did assist in making clothing that was needed quickly. They could also make repairs to clothing. Sewing was a task that was appropriate for a wife to undertake, whose husband had the status of a non-commissioned officer

After 1815, when hostilities with France were over, the lives of Thomas and Elisabeth became more stable. The militia was moved onto a peacetime footing, assembling only periodically for training and exercises. One of the few departures from this routine occurred when the regiment was called out with the Perthshire Yeomanry to suppress a riot at Brechin in 1820. On several occasions after 1815, reductions were made in the permanent staff of the militia but Thomas was exempted from them. His normal station remained at Perth.

When Thomas died in 1835, Elisabeth, aged fifty one, was given a widow's pension paid as a lump sum annually, for his service. Had that pension been insufficient for the household, (with two young children at home in 1835), she may have obtained earnings from being a seamstress. She may also have been given financial support from the older children still living at home. By 1851, she had left Perth and joined her son George, a law clerk, in Glasgow. No record of her death has been found.

Agnes Muric

Agnes Murie was born in 1815, in Perth. In 1838, she married Perth-born James Pearson, a jeweller, and they had five daughters and one son between 1839 and 1854. It was usual for a jeweller to serve an apprenticeship of seven years, beginning at the age of fourteen. Craftsmen such as jewellers were often following in their fathers' footsteps. The craft of the jeweller was interchangeable with that of the silversmith, goldsmith and watchmaker. They employed special tools and equipment to make jewellery and to insert jewels into the watch mechanism to help reduce friction. Engaged in fiddly meticulous work for long hours, they were employed in small workshops where some specialisation was common.

James Pearson was in a highly specialised trade but when employers had no work for them, migration became necessary for these tradesmen. Jewellers were amongst the old established crafts which had formed trade societies that from their beginnings had assisted members to find work around the country – amongst other functions. Temporary accommodation and admission to a job was offered to these 'tramping artisans', who had to keep travelling until they found a vacancy. The records show that James left Perth for Edinburgh about 1840, moved to Inverness about 1846, to Glasgow about 1853 and had returned to Perth in 1855. Within each of these towns, James may have had several different employers and only left the town when it could offer no further work to him.

Agnes became a widow, aged forty in 1855 when James died, aged forty three. His death is a mystery, with the most probable cause being an infectious disease, epidemics of which, periodically swept through the towns. There was no financial provision for widowed mothers at this time and so earnings from work became imperative for Agnes. The *Perth Directory* for 1855/56 listed her as a seamstress at her home address, which suggests that immediately after James's death, she was seeking work from the public, and may have been taking in work as a seamstress prior to that. Finding the income to pay all the bills including rent could only have been very difficult. It is very probable that the children had greater responsibility thrust upon them to contribute to their upkeep, which for the older ones required them to leave home to find work. Of Agnes's six children in 1861, only two were still living at home with her, two were domestic servants at other addresses. The records suggest that one child had died and they are silent about the whereabouts of another.

Agnes's employment as a seamstress was common for widows with children in Victorian Britain. Sewing was a means to support their families and it enabled them to stay at home with their children rather than be employed in domestic service, which was the main alternative for them. It may be that having learned to sew from her mother, Agnes also earned her living from it before marriage rather than from employment in the principal industry in Perth, textiles. If Agnes, after marriage, made and repaired clothes for her own children, which was usual for wives, then she was also able to deploy these skills on a remunerative basis. Seamstresses would take in work and often make simple garments or restyle old ones. They played an important role in the provision of cheap clothing outside the retail trade. As such, Agnes either worked for herself or worked for the many small businesses sub-contracting work. Many seamstresses worked at home sewing ready-made clothing for very low piece rates. They worked long hours and for meagre earnings. The sheer number of women willing to use a needle and their general lack of alternative employment made their labour cheap and expendable. Seamstresses in outworking were vulnerable to employers who could withhold or delay payment if work was deemed substandard. It was also common practice for seamstresses to have to pay for their own thread, needles, candles in addition to heating and the costs of collecting and returning the work.

Whist the job of seamstress enabled widows like Agnes to earn a living, it created a sweatshop system for many who worked very long hours for low wages. Layoffs due to seasonal demand were common. Pay and conditions remained bad throughout the 1800s. Needlework confined women to the home to do the dull repetitive work of plying the needle. There were also some health hazards for seamstresses which arose from the working conditions and long hours. Eyesight could be damaged from the close work in poor light and bodily posture could be adversely affected from the position adopted from prolonged hours of sewing.

Having started as a seamstress working for herself, by 1861, Agnes was employed as an upholstery seamstress. Making clothes remained a manual operation until the middle of the 1800s. After 1856, the sewing machine came into widespread use and changed the work of seamstresses. From first using a sewing machine to make and repair clothes, Agnes then became an upholstery seamstress.

When all the children had left home, Agnes moved from Perth

to Dundee, where she was living in 1871. Dundee offered better employment opportunities than Perth for it was a growing city with a larger labour market. For Agnes, it also offered the chance of being near her family for her daughters Agnes and Allison were already living there and could offer her the companionship that she had lost when all the children had left home in Perth. In her later years in Dundee, Agnes lived with her daughter, Allison. When she stopped earning her living as a seamstress she became housekeeper in the home that she and Allison shared. She died in 1898, aged eighty three.

Agnes Pearson

Agnes Pearson was born in Edinburgh in 1841. Her childhood years were there and in Inverness. Agnes left home in Perth after her father died in 1855 and was working as a domestic servant in Westgate, Newcastle on Tyne in 1861. Her younger sister, Margaret similarly had left home for domestic service in Perth in 1861. In the 1800s, employment for women in Scotland was overwhelmingly concentrated in domestic service, agriculture, clothing and textiles.

Agnes's employer in 1861, John Howison, was also the Northumberland County Architect and Surveyor and had sufficient income to employ nineteen year old Agnes and another female domestic servant who was of the same age. The household that Agnes and her peer served was only four in number. The work of female domestic servants often included the use of the needle for sewing and mending. After leaving Newcastle on Tyne, Agnes later moved to Aberdeen to work as a seamstress. It was here in 1869 that she married Stewart Fenwick, a currier and they moved to Dundee.

Agnes may have continued to work as a seamstress after her marriage. The census between 1871 and 1901 did not record her as employed but it has been established that this population count seriously under-recorded the extent of women's' work. One survey by a voluntary organisation in Dundee found that about half of all working class wives were working, which contrasted with the census figure for the city of less than a quarter. Many working class wives took work as and when it was available in order to eke out the family income. In Dundee, Agnes and Stewart eventually had six children to support. In the city, married women's paid work was commonplace. Therefore, it seems probable that Agnes continued in her occupation as a seamstress, after her marriage. The rest of her life after marriage is described in chapter 7. Her daughter, Agnes Murie Fenwick was also a stitcher or more specifically a leather machinist and her life is also described in chapter 7.

Chapter 9

Ferry Folk

Broughty Ferry is a prosperous suburb, four miles from the centre of Dundee on the river Tay. It is known colloquially as the ferry. It has a long maritime history and was a fishing village, and then a town before it was incorporated into Dundee in 1913. Eva Mary Ferguson's maternal forebears were natives of Broughty Ferry. They were, therefore, ferry folk. Eva's earliest recorded maternal forebear was Elspeth Watson in 1652. She was succeeded, in order of descent, by Margaret Lanceman, Janet Webster, Janet Young, Catherine Kidd, Margaret Knight, Isabella Webster and Margaret Brown. Margaret Brown was born in Stornoway and lived largely in Dundee. Eva Mary Ferguson, born in Dundee, lived all her life there.

Broughty Ferry's origins were a ferry that crossed from the north side of the river Tay, to the south side. That service commenced during the reign of Robert the Bruce (1274-1329). The ferry travelled the shortest distance between Angus and Fife on the Tay estuary. At this time, the villages on the northern and southern sides of the Tay, at either end of the ferry service, were both known as Portincraig. When Broughty Ferry was emerging as a settlement, population movement in the countryside was high but much of the movement was over short distances of a few kilometres. Therefore it is quite possible that Eva Ferguson's maternal forebears were inhabitants of Broughty Ferry from its beginnings. A castle was built about 1498 on the northern side of the Tay and the name Portincraig fell out of use. The two settlements on the opposite sides of the Tay came to be known as North Ferry and South Ferry. Within North Ferry, the inhabited areas around the Castle came to be known as West Ferry (in Dundee parish) and East Ferry (in Monifieth parish). The name Broughty Ferry eventually came into use instead of North Ferry and the name Tayport came into use instead of South Ferry.

Broughty Ferry was the seat of a fishing population for hundreds of years. At the end of the 1100s, charters were granted to the feudal land owners in Monifieth parish which conferred on them fishing rights. They in turn permitted the common people to fish legitimately but the latter were obliged to give some of their catch to the estate owners. Salmon, herring and shellfish were amongst the seafood that was harvested by local inhabitants. Generally, most fishing around the coasts of Scotland was primarily for subsistence and commercial activity developed later. Coastal dwellers who were not wholly engaged in fishing combined it with other activities such as seafaring and peasantry. Specialisation in fishing through the establishment of fishing villages on the east coast of Scotland appears to have started generally after 1700.

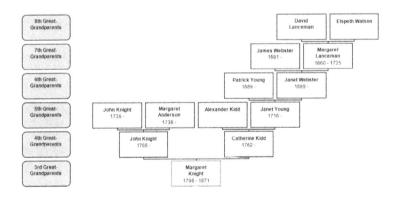

Elspeth Watson

Eva Ferguson's earliest maternal forebear, Elspeth Watson, was married to David Lanceman in 1652 in Dundee. They lived in the village of West Ferry, in the parish of Dundee. They became parents to two children. For the peasant population living by the coast, seafaring and fishing were a part of their lives together with agricultural work and spinning of linen and wool. An account from 1678 describes a traditional practice at Broughty Ferry to catch the salmon when they made their seasonal return from the sea. The inhabitants were in the habit of kindling fires on the banks of the Tay at night and while the fish swam towards the light, the people were ready to pierce them with spears and other sharp instruments. Great quantities of salmon were caught using this method, enough for some to be sold outside the district. Perhaps Elspeth Watson and David Lanceman participated in this custom.

Margaret Lanceman

Margaret Lanceman was born in Broughty Ferry in 1660 and married James Webster in 1681. They became parents to eleven children in fifteen years. It is probable that James Webster combined agricultural work with being a fisherman or a seafarer. Fishing and sea-faring were at this time, as they had been for centuries, an important aspect of everyday life in the village. Sea-faring could include deviant behaviour as illustrated by two historical accounts from church disciplinary records. In 1690, two fishers admitted their guilt in catching salmon on a Sunday. In the same year, another two men admitted their guilt in putting out boats to salvage shipwrecked timber on a Sunday.

Janet Webster

Janet Webster was born in 1689 and married Patrick Young in 1715. They had twelve children in nineteen years. Patrick Young was a shipmaster which means that he was a captain or owner of a boat. The maritime tradition of Broughty Ferry was strong before, during and after the lives of Janet and Patrick. This tradition was demonstrated by the parish church at Monifieth village that served

Broughty Ferry. The building existed between the 1200s and 1812 when it was demolished for replacement by a new church. In the building that was demolished, there was a replica of a full sailing ship that was suspended from the roof. The replica was ornamented by a figure of Neptune and other nautical symbols. The significance of the tradition was also shown by the Old Graveyard at Broughty Ferry where inscriptions of the internments made between 1689 and 1861 suggest that approximately a third of the graves were for shipmasters. Although Broughty Ferry had no harbour (until 1870), it was nonetheless a centre for maritime activity for years prior to that. This was helped by the deep water where vessels could anchor and by the beaches where smaller boats could be hauled up.

The seafaring tradition of Broughty Ferry was already well established by 1696. For in that year, of all the one hundred and twenty three vessels using the port of Dundee, fifteen were registered at Broughty Ferry. Small vessels may have been built at Broughty Ferry for centuries. In 1841, they were occasionally built there where the nature of the shore permitted them to be launched into deep water. Broughty Ferry was very close to the port of Dundee which was the centre of much coastal trade in the area. Many boats ferried goods between ships and shore and also delivered goods to coastal towns and villages in Angus and Fife. Passengers were also ferried between Broughty Ferry and Tayport in Fife. Small boats - which could go upriver or land on a beach - were widely used in preference to the inland alternative of wheeled packhorses since they could carry larger loads and use the wind as a source of power. Smuggling was not uncommon and the goods involved were items such as coal, salt, timber and wines.

Janet Young

Janet Young was born in 1716 and married Alexander Kidd in 1745. They had nine children in fourteen years. By this time, fishing in Broughty Ferry was probably more of a commercial activity than hitherto. As such, fishermen's wives assisted their husbands by baiting the lines and dealing with the catch as well as undertaking the household chores.

Fishermen in Broughty Ferry caught salmon by net and coble. This method of fishing for salmon had been in use since the 1200s, with little change in the interval. A long net was released from the stern of a small rowing boat (a coble) to surround the fish and then drawn ashore onto a beach. The salmon were then preserved in wooden barrels with salt and were exported to countries like the Netherlands and France. The salmon catch was also sold to London from 1778.

Catherine Kidd

Catherine Kidd was born in 1762 and she married John Knight, a fisherman, in 1784. They had eight children in eighteen years. By the end of the 1700s, fishermen in Broughty Ferry had constructed cottages near the shore line and had also put huts on the beach. The community into which Catherine Kidd was born was made up of a small number of families who were bound together by inter-marriage. The fishing families shared the same surnames, with the Websters and Knights being two of the nine common surnames. In 1798, there were three large sail boats operating out of Broughty Ferry which caught haddock, sole, cod, whiting and plaice. Lobster and crab were also caught. The population of the village was approximately four hundred inhabitants. It grew rapidly after that, as did the numbers engaged in fishing for a living. However, the fishing community remained distinct from the wider community with little intermarriage between the two.

Lines were used for the white fish in the traditional fishing grounds of the Tay Estuary and St Andrews Bay. The white fish included haddock, cod, ling, flounders, sole, whiting, plaice, skate and turbot. The vicinity of Bell Rock was popular. These fishing grounds could involve the fishermen sitting in an open boat all night. During the herring season, the fishermen would follow the shoals from as far north as Shetland and as far south as Suffolk. The lives of the fishermen were hard and rigorous. About fifty families were dependent on white fishing for their living by the 1830s. The boats used were usually crewed by six but in summer, larger boats were used for herring fishing in Northern Scotland.

The community to which Catherine Kidd belonged was a very cohesive one. By tradition, crew members of each fishing boat, (usually numbering six) owned shares in it. The crew of the boat were co-owners and shared the profits from fishing. If a man married outside the fishing community, he would forfeit his shares. Women equally, were not expected to choose husbands who were outsiders. When a man was lost from a boat, the crew continued to carry his lines for a year and gave the share of the profits to his widow and children. This convention recognised that fishing was the most dangerous peacetime occupation of all. Fishing relied on the combined labour of the family unit and customs were followed which supported the co-operative kin based character of the work. Thus Catherine Kidd and the other fishermen's wives had a very important economic role.

Fishermen's wives had the task of disposing of the merchandise caught by their husbands. Some preparation of the fish for sale was required after which the wives with creels (baskets) full of fresh fish fitted to their backs hawked them around Dundee and villages adjacent to Broughty Ferry. To carry a creel of fish, wives used a broad leather belt that rested forwards on their foreheads to support the creel on their backs. Carrying the fish around on their backs was hard work. The fish were sold by calling door to door and bargaining over the price.

In addition to selling the fish, the fishermen's wives were responsible, with their children, for baiting the hooks for the lines. This involved digging up lugworm, for example, with a spade and depositing them in a bucket. The hooks on the line had to be knotted and after its collection, the hooks baited. Each line to be baited could include over seven hundred hooks. The fishermen's wives were also kept busy repairing the fishing nets. The nets had to be kept in good condition to catch the salmon. This activity was usually conducted with the neighbours and so also provided an opportunity for gossiping. A further source of food both for sale and family consumption was shellfish which was collected from the beaches. The shellfish included mussels, periwinkles, dog whelks, limpets and edible crabs. Of course there were domestic chores also for which the fishermen's wives were responsible. The cottages inhabited by the fishing families were one-roomed in which nets and other equipment had to be stored.

One aspect of life in the 1700s that was fairly common, particularly for those living in coastal communities, was smuggling. It was widespread on the east coast of Scotland throughout the century (and much of the rest of Britain too). Holland and Scandinavia were the principal sources of smuggling trade in the Tay area. Illicit goods from abroad included French brandy, Dutch gin, wine, tea and tobacco. In the Tay area, much of the smuggling was of salt for preserving fish locally. Huge quantities entered the country illegally. Salt was heavily taxed and the regulations governing salt imports were extremely complicated, which was an incentive to ignore them.

The motivation for fishermen to smuggle in Broughty Ferry is suggested by an observation in the *Old Statistical Account*. It was noted that fish were caught in such a small quantity they afforded a very scanty and precarious subsistence. Therefore smuggling goods into the country, was a way to make ends meet. Moreover, it seems that few outside Westminster saw anything wrong with smuggling.

In taking part in smuggling, fishermen signalled the vessel carrying contraband to arrange a meeting point a few miles offshore where they would collect the illicit goods in their fishing boat or boats. The contraband would then be ferried to the shore and hidden in a suitable location, possibly being buried on a beach where it could be collected later for further transportation and distribution. Smaller boats were used for contraband when the risk of an open landing was too great or the coast was unsuitable for a large vessel to land goods. Women played a part in smuggling in peripheral ways. They retailed smuggled salt, hidden in their clothing, to local women.

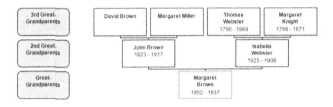

Margaret Knight

Margaret Knight was born in 1798 and aged twenty seven, she married thirty five year old Thomas Webster in 1825. They had ten children in fifteen years. By the time of their marriage, Thomas's experience as a seafarer extended beyond fishing.

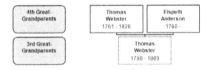

Thomas had, as a boy, started to fish with his father at Broughty Ferry. From there at the age of thirteen, he joined the Sea Fencibles and served from 1803 until 1810, when they were disbanded. The Sea Fencibles were formed during the Napoleonic War to defend the coastline against the enemy, France. The Sea Fencible service or Corps of Sea Fencibles was a part-time organisation of volunteers recruited from fishermen and boatmen who were under the command of serving or retired naval officers. It was formed for local defence and mobilised in case of invasion or emergency. It was started in 1798 to help prepare for the defence of the eastern and southern coastline of England from invasion by the French. In 1803 the Corps was extended to include the whole of the British coastline which was divided into forty districts, one of which was Angus.

Whist a seaman with the Sea Fencibles at Broughty Ferry, Thomas served with his father as did other father and sons. Whilst the age of thirteen years appears very young for military service today, it was not so remarkable in 1803, because it was customary for many boys to join the navy at twelve and some did so even earlier.

Volunteering for the Corps usually followed adverts in local newspapers inviting those interested to attend a meeting for enrolment that was held locally. Volunteers for the Sea Fencibles were granted immunity both from conscription into the militia and impressment into the Royal Navy. The ordinary seamen who constituted the Sea Fencibles wore a distinctive uniform (like the Royal Navy) and were paid a shilling per day and given food and drink when on duty. There was no shortage of recruits for the Sea Fencibles. They were required for duty for about a day a week. In the event of an alarm, the men would make to a rendevous point and proceed to patrol a specific length of coast. They would also assist with coastal signal stations, were trained in the use of arms and in the handling of armed coastal craft.

Broughty Ferry, with Arbroath and Montrose constituted the Angus District of the Sea Fencibles, which was under the command of several officers, one of whom was Captain John Rufsel. The seamen that Thomas Webster served alongside numbered from twelve to fifteen on their days of duty and went by the names of Knight, Anderson, Kidd, Norie, Lorimer, Sime and Gaull. These names were typical Broughty Ferry names. As a volunteer in the Sea Fencibles, Thomas Webster was one of about twenty thousand men tasked with protecting the coast of Great Britain.

It is easy to imagine why Thomas Webster volunteered for the Sea Fencibles in Broughty Ferry during the Napoleonic war. He was following the example of his father and other local fishermen and meeting the expectations of the community to which he belonged. Patriotism was exhorted at the time and was manifested by volunteering for some form of military service. Had he and his father failed to volunteer, they might have been ostracised by the community. In any case, the prospect of joining the Corps offered an opportunity to be recognised as an adult, which at the age of thirteen was an appealing idea. Entry into the Sea Fencibles also offered him the chance of great adventure and excitement from helping to defend the coastline from invasion. A principal incentive for many who volunteered for the Corps was that they were given a certificate which protected them from impressment. Impressment was commonplace around all the ports at this time and was a principal source of recruitment for the Royal Navy. Impressment was limited to those between the ages of eighteen years and fifty five but the limits were frequently ignored. Although immunity from impressment may have been of little importance to Thomas Webster when he first volunteered, it may have become increasingly important as he grew older. In volunteering for the Sea Fencibles, Thomas Webster was assured of the friendship, company and support of male members of his local community. A further reward he could rely on was the regular payment of a shilling for each day of duty, a helpful contribution to the family budget.

On duty, the Sea Fencibles patrolled the local coast and were trained in manoeuvring their boats and drilled in the use of pikes and cannons and ammunition. The cannons, gunpowder and ammunition were provided by the Admiralty and delivered to vessels (the optimum size was one hundred and fifty tons), which were donated by local merchants and ship owners.

The Sea Fencibles were disbanded nationally in 1810, because the threat of a French invasion had disappeared. The disbandment brought an important phase of Thomas Webster's life to an end, at the age of nineteen. He then served in the Royal Navy in which he rose to the rank of boatswain. The war with Napoleonic France was still being fought and men were still needed for the Royal Navy. Thomas either volunteered for the Royal Navy or was conscripted into it. The latter course was possible for the disbandment of the Sea Fencibles meant that he had lost his immunity from impressment. As either a volunteer or a conscript, he was an attractive recruit to the Royal Navy for he had experience as a mariner from a young age including six years' in the Sea Fencibles.

When Thomas Webster joined the Royal Navy during the war with France, its strength was one hundred and fifty thousand men and its fleet numbered eight hundred and fifty vessels, all powered by sail. Steam power was introduced into the Navy in 1849. Life in the Navy was a very organised and disciplined way of life aboard ship. There were many punishments for misdemeanours that were committed. Boatswains, had responsibilities for rigging, sails, boats, anchors and all cabling. The rank of boatswain was a senior rating and classed with chief petty officers and petty officers. To have attained the rank, the holder had progressed to it after having shown competence both as an ordinary seaman, then able seaman, for several years. Most ships had a large number of petty officers, for example the largest; a hundred and ten gun ship with eight hundred and twenty nine men had seventy eight petty officers.

Because he joined the Navy in 1810 or after, Thomas Webster benefited from improvements both in nutrition and hygiene that had been introduced from the start of the century. Vegetables were available as was citrus fruit to prevent scurvy. On the debit side of naval life were accidents aboard ship, which were frequent, with falls from mast and rigging being most common. Wherever he was, gunnery practice was an important element of daily duty for men aboard. The Royal Navy had world-wide responsibilities but where he was stationed is a secret. It is possible that he served in home waters. His service in the Coastguard from 1825 may have been a continuation of his Royal Naval service combatting smuggling. For prior to 1822, the three services that preceded the Coastguard had revenue cruisers that were crewed by the Royal Navy and that custom continued for several years after the formation of the Coastguard in 1822. Their purpose was to combat smuggling and collect revenue that was owed. There were six Navy ships assigned to Coastguard service in Scotland which were based at Leith. It is possible therefore, that Thomas Webster may have gained some experience of combatting smuggling from service in these cruisers which facilitated his admission to the Coastguard subsequently.

After their marriage in 1825, Margaret and Thomas, later in the year, became parents of the first of their ten children. At the very end of 1825, Thomas was appointed as a boatman in the Coastguard at Auchmithie, Angus. The practice of the Coastguard was to transfer their men away from their home locations and later in their service, to different locations. The aim of this practice was to avoid collusion. There was a fear that if the men of the Coastguard were too well acquainted with the local people, they might connive in smuggling. Thomas and Margaret therefore had to surrender their attachment to Broughty Ferry for the length of his service in the Coastguard. Margaret's life from here on did not include helping with fishing or the catch. Instead, her activities were domestic chores and child rearing. The loss that was experienced by Thomas and Margaret on him joining the Coastguard was recovered on his retirement from the service in 1848. They returned to their home village which by now had become a town.

Why did Thomas Webster leave the Royal Navy for the Coastguard? Two factors were important. The Coastguard usually offered a better salary than was paid by the Navy and did not usually require long absences from families. In the Coastguard, there were family quarters attached to a land based Coastguard station. Absence from these quarters was only for occasional periods of drill of ten to fourteen days on board ship. In contrast, in the Royal Navy, absence from home could be for long periods when ships put to sea. Nonetheless, the change from the Royal Navy to the Coastguard represented continuity for Thomas and Margaret for their way of life was largely determined by him being in military service. The Coastguard was officered by serving royal navy officers and the ratings were often men who had served in the Royal Navy. By 1839 there were over four thousand five hundred and fifty three Coastguards.

Thomas was posted to the Auchmithie station near Arbroath initially and then in 1832 to the Usan station in the parish of Craig, near Montrose. At Usan, the neighbouring households to Thomas and Margaret were the families of the Coastguard and fishermen. The Coastguard establishment at Usan station was six, of which there was a chief officer, a chief boatman, a commissioned boatman and 3 boatmen. Boatmen were employed as oarsmen.

Prior to the Coastguard station at Usan, in the nearby village of Ferryden, smuggling wine and other contraband was a lucrative source of income for a community that was very dependent on fishing. At one time, the smuggling of gin and brandy from Holland prevailed to a great extent and great quantities of Highland whisky were brought into the parish by illicit traders. The establishment of the Coastguard completely stopped the practice of smuggling.

Thomas Webster retired from the Coastguard on a pension in 1848 and he and Margaret and the family returned to their community in Broughty Ferry. The Broughty Ferry that Thomas Webster returned to was much changed from the little fishing village of his childhood. The population had swelled and visitors and holiday makers had increased in number, especially as a result of the opening of the Dundee to Arbroath railway in 1838. Many of the better off chose to escape living in industrial Dundee in preference for the healthier environment of Broughty Ferry. Thomas Webster died in 1869 aged seventy nine and Margaret Knight, died in 1871, aged seventy two.

Isabella Webster

Isabella Webster was born in 1825 and her early years were on the Angus coast where her father was stationed in the Coastguard. Isabella came of age in the parish of Craig where the economy was based on agriculture and fishing. Agricultural production was grain of all kinds. Potatoes, cabbages and turnips were also grown. Some of the land was used for cattle and sheep rearing. For females in this parish other than fishing families, the most likely jobs they held were therefore either as domestic servants, agricultural labourers or a combination of the two. In 1848, Isabella married a native of the parish, John Brown, a stonemason, who had learned his trade from his father, a stone mason employed as a farm servant. Isabella and John had three children in seven years.

There were quarries in various parts of the parish which provided amygdaloidal trap rock which was commonly employed in building in the parish although it was not suitable for facing the doors and windows of dwelling houses. Masons were one of the occupations of agricultural employees. Masonry was considered a skilled trade, with status and income to match. Many stonemasons developed their skills and later became architects and civil engineers. John Brown followed a similar path for he later diversified his work from stonemasonry to building in general, at which he was successful.

Stonemasons, like other artisans at this time, were accustomed to travelling long distances for work and John was no exception. After his marriage, in 1849, accompanied by Isabella, he travelled to the Orkney island of Graemsay and in 1851, to Hebridean island of Lewis. At both these places he was employed on the construction of on-shore lighthouses and associated buildings. John's sojourn in these remote islands was through his employment by Alan Stevenson of the Stevenson family of civil engineers. Alan Stevenson, was the Chief Engineer to the Commissioners of the Northern Lighthouse Board between 1844 and 1854 and he was responsible for the design and construction of ten new lighthouses. He was also Clerk of

Works to the Board and was responsible for ensuring every detail of the lighthouses were checked and executed correctly. It was the practice of Alan Stevenson to give two years guaranteed work to the workers that he hired to build lighthouses. He employed very little local labour generally, and masons were a significant occupational group in the labour force he hired. Just as labour was imported to build the lighthouses, some stone also was imported if the local quarried stone was considered not adequate for all building purposes.

Graemsay lies at the northern entrance to Scapa Flow between Stromness and Hoy. It is one and a half miles long and one mile broad. Its total population when John and Isabella stayed there was about two hundred and thirty people. Hoy High & Hoy Low Lighthouses were built on Graemsay to act as leading lights to the western approaches of Hoy Sound, to clear the submerged Bow Rock of Hoy and Kirk Rocks of Warbeth. The construction of the lighthouses also included the construction of single storey cottages for the keepers, sheds, outbuildings, and a slipway and perimeter wall. The two lighthouses were completed and in operation in1851.

With the completion of the lighthouses in 1851, John and Isabella moved to Arnish Point, near Stornoway, Lewis. Arnish Point, was the site of a lighthouse at the entrance to the bay in which Stornoway was situated. The lighthouse was completed and lit in 1853. Built with it, were keepers' cottages. John and Isabella lived at Arnish Point outside the town of Stornoway with its population of three thousand. Arnish Point was rough moorland and positioned at some distance from Stornoway. Indeed it was so remote a location that there were difficulties in finding a contractor to do the job. It is not clear what accommodation John Brown and family occupied at Arnish Point and it seems that the site was uninhabited prior to the building of the lighthouse. It may be that as with the other lighthouses that were built at the time, workmen's cottages or keepers cottages were built first of all, as shelter for the builders. An additional adversity that they had to cope with was the uncongenial climate that was very damp.

In 1854, after completion of the lighthouse at Arnish Point, John and Isabella moved to Monifieth, where they lived for the next ten years. They were near to Isabella's family, who had returned to Broughty Ferry, on her father's retirement from the Coastguard. In Monfieth, John started his own business which prospered. Their prosperity was shared by their neighbours who in 1861 included a cabinet maker, an insurance agent and a neighbour living on investments who employed a housekeeper and a domestic servant.

John moved his business and home to Dundee in 1864. Dundee was in a period of rapid expansion, so the move was astute for there was plenty of work for a mason and builder. John built houses first in Strathmartine Road when it was in the rural periphery of Dundee prior to its listing as a residential road. Later he also built houses in Provost Road. He retained ownership of these houses and rented them out. He and Isabella occupied one of the houses in Strathmartine Road. John's business also built churches and public buildings. With the growth and diversification of his business, he changed the description of it from mason to builder. Before long the business was large enough to warrant premises that were separate from the home address. John's son David, became his business partner but the partnership came to an end when David died in 1886, aged thirty six. He left behind a wife and daughter. John retired from his business in 1890 but continued as a landlord. His tenants (and neighbours) included his two daughters and their families.

Isabella died in 1906 aged eighty and John died aged ninety three in 1917. John had accumulated wealth over his lifetime from his work as a builder. There was no inventory of his wealth in the will that he left (administered by Trustees that he had appointed) but it is known that he owned thirteen properties in 1915. The will instructed the Trustees to hold the estate for a maximum of five years and to realise the estate at their discretion. The estate was divided principally between his two daughters, Margaret and Isabella. Sums of money were also specified for other members of the family including a generous sum to his son's widow.

Margaret Brown

Margaret Brown was born in Stornoway, Lewis, in 1852 and her childhood was spent in Monifieth and Dundee. After leaving school she became a power loom weaver like her sister. In 1874, she married David Ferguson who was a mechanic in the jute industry. The remainder of her life and the life of her daughter, Eva Mary Ferguson, is described in chapter 10.

Chapter 10

Juteopolis People

Juteopolis is the nickname that the city of Dundee acquired as a result of its domination by the jute industry from the mid-1800s. Prior to its designation as juteopolis, Dundee had a long history of producing wool and then linen. Indeed, its development as a textile town was instrumental in it becoming the jute manufacturing capital of the world. Eva Mary Ferguson's paternal forebears were juteopolis people, for they, like her, lived and worked in Dundee. Her earlier paternal forebears were also inhabitants of Dundee before the city was labelled as juteopolis. Her earliest paternal forebears came to Dundee from Angus.

The early paternal Ferguson forebears, George, John and George (the second), were peasants in rural Angus. George (the second), moved to Dundee and became a handloom weaver in the early 1700s. George's son David (the first), shared his father's occupation whilst linen production was a thriving industry in Dundee. David was succeeded by David (the second), a harbour porter who conveyed goods between warehouses and ships in the harbour in the late 1700s. David's son, James, was a quarryman, when the local quarries supplied stone for the development of Dundee harbour between 1810 and 1836. James's son David (the third), was a mechanic in the team that set up the first jute mill in Calcutta in 1855. His son, David (the fourth) also became a jute mechanic, manager of a jute mill in Calcutta and a self-employed engineer. David's daughter, Eva, was employed in the textile industry and Eva's brother, Harry, followed his father's example as a jute mill manager in Calcutta in 1912.

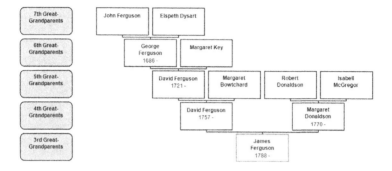

George, John and George (the second)

The Fergusons originated in rural Angus or Forfarshire as it was then known, in the 1600s. In 1690 nine out of ten Scotsmen lived on the land and Scotland was largely a country of peasants. These circumstances suggest that the early Fergusons living in rural Angus were peasants. The peasant population of Scotland performed a multitude of agricultural tasks that included spinning and weaving to help sustain their lives.

George Ferguson married Christian Cantie and in 1656 they had a son in the parish of Mains and Strathmartine. John later moved a few miles to the parish of St Vigeans by Arbroath where he married Elspeth Dysart in 1685. In 1686 John and Elspeth had a son, George (the second).

Around the time of George's birth, movement of population both within rural areas and from rural areas to the towns was normal, particularly among younger people, though often over limited distances. Population movement to the towns tended to be on a regional basis. One important driver of population movement was the pursuit of an apprenticeship. Another driver was that recurring subsistence crises (usually from poor harvests) prompted people to take to the roads in large numbers. George's parish of St Vigeans was only a distance of about twenty miles to Dundee and George found his way there either for better opportunities or merely so he could feed himself and survive. George may have brought with him to Dundee some skills in weaving from his agricultural background.

As one of the big four towns in Scotland and a regional centre that had prospered from textile manufacture, Dundee was attractive to country dwellers who wished to escape from an austere existence. The Dundee that George migrated to had a population of about six thousand. In those days, this size of population was a large town and so was probably a strange place to George, a peasant, when he first arrived there. George became a handloom weaver in Dundee and in 1713 he married Margaret Key. They had six children in twelve years. Throughout Scotland, it was a customary domestic activity for wives to undertake spinning of linen which was then woven by their husbands. Therefore, in George's household, Margaret probably upheld this convention.

Not long after George's marriage, the Old Pretender made a public entry into Dundee on Horseback on 6 January 1716. He was seeking to restore the Stuarts to the throne and he was welcomed by his supporters which included magistrates and gentry. His visit was brief however. Most of the inhabitants of the town were loyal to the House of Hanover and therefore hostile to the visit of James Stuart, son of the deposed King James.

David Ferguson (the first)

David Ferguson (the first), was born in Dundee in 1721. In 1750, at the age of twenty nine, he married Margaret Bowtchard and they had six children in fourteen years. The Dundee that David was born into still had a population of only a few thousand and an economy rooted in the production of linen. In 1707, one million and five hundred thousand yards of linen were made in the town annually. Weaving in Dundee was a long established trade (mainly of wool originally), the guild of weavers having been granted a charter by the town council in 1512. There is plenty of evidence that weavers were organised as a body before that date. The guild of weavers succeeded in ensuring that only Dundee woven yarn was sold in the town until 1751 when their power was broken by Act of Parliament. The guild was composed of the master weavers who were the merchants and employers. David followed his father in becoming a handloom weaver. It is possible that he weaved other fibres for there was some making of cloth from cotton and wool and also coloured thread in Dundee. Linen in David Ferguson's time was Scotland's most important export. David, it seems, was not a master weaver and so he did not acquire the wealth and status that came from that position.

An event of some importance occurred during David's younger years in Dundee - the Jacobite rebellion of 1745. Jacobite rebels numbering six hundred occupied the town for five months. They were in support of the Young Pretender and for restoring the Stuarts to the throne. Only in January 1746 did the magistrates and council, who were opposed to the Stuart cause, succeed in ridding the town of the rebels.

Hand loom weavers like David Ferguson usually occupied one room where there was a hand loom to weave linen. The linen was delivered by a merchant who had bought the linen from the market in Dundee. The linen was sold at the market by housewives who had spun it in their homes in the rural parishes outside Dundee. Towards the end of David's working life, linen that was delivered to weavers was more likely to have been imported from abroad rather than having been produced in rural Angus. If David and his wife Margaret followed custom, she did some of the spinning of linen for him to weave.

David Ferguson (the second)

David (the second), was born in 1757, in Dundee. He married Margaret Donaldson in 1786 and they became the parents of three children over four years. In the 1700s, Dundee was an increasingly important port for both coastal and foreign trade and David became a harbour porter.

The harbour porters fetched and carried goods between the harbour and warehouses that were within easy reach of the waterfront. The main trade was linen for export and flax for import, with other goods also being traded. Much of the foreign trade was with the Eastern Baltic. Accordingly, the harbour porters unloaded timber, iron, tea, hemp, tow, linseed, and coal (mined in Fife) from the ships and stowed them in warehouses and delivered thread, sail cloth, cotton bagging, barley, and wheat to the ships holds in Dundee Harbour. In 1792, one hundred and sixteen vessels belonged to the port of Dundee. Thirty four were employed in the foreign trade and seventy eight in the coastal trade. There were only four berths in 1792 at which loaded vessels were permitted to deliver their cargoes. The enlargement and development of the harbour changed that capacity after 1815.

Dundee was important as a centre for the collection and distribution of a wide range of basic and luxury goods to the surrounding areas. This task was undertaken by carters who were differentiated from the porters by owning a horse and cart or waggon but the two occupations collaborated in the work of loading and unloading goods. Carters transported goods between the harbour and destinations that were further afield or where the goods were greater in quantity. The number of carters rose commensurately with the expansion of trade. In 1746 there was only one carter in Dundee but by 1799 there were one hundred and thirty fully employed. Porters were numerically less. In 1824 licensed carters were one hundred and nine whilst licensed porters were eighty.

To become a harbour porter, a license had to be obtained from the magistrates acting for the town council which managed the harbour until 1815. An applicant had to satisfy them that he was a proper person to do the job. He was then admitted to a register of porters for which he had to pay an admission fee and to wear at all times a badge. He also had to keep on him a copy of the regulations of porters to show to his employers. These regulations made by the town council listed what he could and could not do as a porter. They specified the sums that he could charge for carrying different goods of different weights on journeys between the harbour and warehouses in different parts of the town (and vice versa). Weighing goods to decide the appropriate charge to be levied was an important part of the job of a porter. He could lose his licence and job if he seriously breached the regulations.

As a harbour porter, David was a member of a fraternity. The porters formed a friendly society, the Dundee Harbour Porters. In 1779 it made a loan of £50 to the nine incorporated trades of Dundee. The society's primary purpose was to give financial support to members who were in difficulty and to their widows.

In addition to payment for the goods carried, porters were also paid 'plank money'. This was a fee that the porters charged for the use of planks to board ships for moving goods in and out of the holds. It is probable that David was hired by the day by a gang master or by a merchant. For very heavy loads, he may have worked with three other porters and used poles and chains for the task. The regulations stated that a porter might carry, for example, coal or another commodity, of ten and a half stones (or sixty six kilograms) for certain distances for which he received prescribed payments. Portering was hard work and porters needed a considerable amount of carbohydrate as fuel – much of which they got from drinking. The regulations for porters specified that plank money was for ale. However, heavy drinking caused intoxication which affected their work. Minutes of meetings of the porters' friendly society showed that fines were regularly imposed on members as a punishment for drunkenness at work and for absence from work as a result of drunkenness. Drunkenness was an occupational disease for the porters.

The Dundee of which David was an inhabitant was a thriving place, and the population grew accordingly from over twelve thousand in 1775 to twenty six thousand in 1800. The Dundee that he lived in was a place of narrow streets, houses that were close together, with families often in possession of single rooms only, in houses that they shared with other families. There was a lack both of recreational areas and public institutions such as schools and a library. There was only a grammar school.

James Ferguson

James Ferguson was born in Dundee in 1788. In 1818, he married Ann Doig and they became the parents of two children. After their marriage, they left Dundee and moved to Lochee, a village on the outskirts of the city.

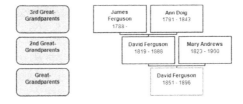

James worked as a quarryman. Two of Dundee's quarries were made from two small hills, the Corbie and Windmill. Until they were quarried away early in the 1800s, the development of Dundee was compressed in a long linear manner with the market at the centre. After 1810, the quarries in Lochee, supplied large quantities of cheap stone for the city that were required for the expansion of the docks and harbour. Prior to 1810, the harbour had limited facilities which could not accommodate vessels of any considerable draught. The harbour was lacking in both size and safety, apparently. The Harbour Commissioners determined to improve matters. Between 1815 and 1830, a wet-dock, with a graving-dock attached to it, was constructed, the tide harbour was deepened and extended, sea-walls and additional quays were built, and various other improvements were made. The harbour was renewed and extended with most improvements finished by 1836. Therefore, as a quarryman, James's lifetime work and earnings was probably an outcome of the development of Dundee harbour.

As a quarryman, James's life was one of hard physical labour, for long hours, on little pay. There was no cutting machinery in use in quarries during most of his working life so the pickaxe was the primary tool. Work outdoors in all the elements was customary and there was also exposure to the risk of accidents inherent in the industry. There was no or little trade union organisation in the industry at this time. In Lochec, there were several quarries that flourished including one owned by the Harbour Commissioners. Whilst the most numerous occupational group in Lochee, by far, was textile employees, masons and their labourers were a lesser but significant group. The textile industry in Lochee was a large employer, particularly of women which suggests that James's wife Ann was probably so employed.

Lochee in James's life-time was an industrial village and like Dundee it had experienced rapid industrialisation and commensurate population growth in the 1800s. A consequence of these changes was that the housing stock, which was two and one storey cottages, became seriously overcrowded. (Tenements were built later in the century). Slum conditions were created just as they were in Dundee. There was an inadequate water supply and a lack of the most elementary forms of public hygiene. Low wages resulted in an inadequate diet and lowered resistance to disease. Outbreaks of infectious diseases, particularly cholera, typhus and tuberculosis, were common. One typhus outbreak occurred in 1843 and James's wife, Ann, aged fifty two, was a fatal victim. James survived her by a few years.

David Ferguson (the third)

David Ferguson (the third) was born in 1819 in Lochee. Lochee is now a suburb of Dundee but then it was a large outlying village but closely connected to the city. In 1843, he married Mary Andrews and between 1844 and 1856, they became the parents of seven children, one of whom did not survive childhood. David and Mary left Lochee for Dundee about 1848.

In Lochee, the principal employment opportunities for David were in the textile industry. Linen production had long been a domestic industry there just as it had been in neighbouring Dundee and from the early 1800s, mechanisation of the industry was occurring. So flax spinning mills were built and driven by steam engines. Factories were built for weaving with hand looms being superseded by power looms. Linen production was complemented by the use of other fibres, most significantly jute. Eventually, there were three textile manufacturers in Lochee, the largest and most notable of which was Cox Brothers. Their Camperdown Linen Works, completed between 1845 and 1850 and occupying eighteen acres, was a massive establishment which incorporated all of the textile processes and employed over three thousand people. Linen was eventually discarded for jute by Cox Brothers but many firms in the district of Dundee manufactured both. The machinery at the Camperdown Linen Works was of the latest and most improved construction and was made on the premises. In 1845, weaving, driven by steam power, started at Cox Brothers.

During his adult working life, David was a mechanic variously described in the records as a machine maker, engine smith, mechanic (fitter) and power loom mechanic. He made, installed, maintained and repaired machinery, including steam engines in the textile industry. His start in the industry was most probably as a child performing simple tasks. For the experience of thousands of children in Lochee and Dundee was that they were employed in the industry to undertake simple work for a low wage. Thus machines were packed closer together because children under nine years, being so small, would work as 'pickers', cleaning dust from beneath the machines. In some mills in Dundee and district in the 1820s, children worked an eighteen or nineteen hour day. In the spinning mills and weaving factories, they could later progress from unskilled employment to more skilled occupations. The job of being a mechanic was learned from first-hand experience of working with machinery.

Mechanisation of the textile industry was in its early stages when David began work. To become a mechanic rather than settle for a lesser skilled occupation called for motivation and the ability to acquire appropriate expertise. As a mechanic in the industry, the financial rewards were much greater than for the other trades such as winders, tenters, lappers, warpers, and calenderers. The mechanics were the aristocrats of labour within the textile industry in Dundee. They were expected to ensure that the machinery was always working well and to repair it immediately, if necessary. They were also expected to secure alterations and improvements in the working of the machinery so that their employers maintained competitiveness within the textile industry. The mills and factories all constantly sought to secure improvements in the operation of their machinery.

David was amongst the small party of mechanics and overseers who travelled to Calcutta, Bengal, in 1855 to establish the first spinning mill there. The venture to Calcutta was promoted by George Ackland an English entrepreneur. Calcutta was chosen because it was in the centre of the jute growing area of Bengal. George Ackland arranged for jute preparing machinery to be supplied by the Douglas Foundry of Dundee and for a Dundee mill expert to start and run the mill. The expert was Robert Finlay who had been manager at the Coldside Mill of James Neish. Many Victorian artisans found that when work ended they could only secure re-employment by travelling the country. For a small number their search for work could take them abroad. It was customary for some of the skilled workers in Dundee's jute industry to travel to Barrow in Furness for a spell and then to return to Dundee. Therefore, David's journey to work in India was not wholly exceptional. For Victorian artisans, travelling to obtain work also offered opportunities to learn about the world beyond the boundaries of the local parish. In being appointed to the team destined for Calcutta, David had to satisfy his employer that he had the personal qualities and technical knowledge that made him suitable for this new enterprise. There may also have been some financial or other reward given for this assignment. There was already traffic between Dundee and Calcutta which began when jute had first been directly shipped to Dundee from Calcutta in 1840. A fleet of between seventy and eighty fully rigged vessels eventually travelled regularly between the two places. The journey for David to Calcutta by sailing ship (via the Cape of Good Hope) took about one hundred and four days.

George Ackland's Rishra spinning mill was opened in 1855. Not very long after it had been established, in 1857, the Indian Mutiny occurred. It included a mutiny at Barrackpore which was not far from Rishra. Fearful that there was a threat to his property, George Ackland requested an armed guard from the military authorities but it was refused. So he hired some seamen from a sailors' home in Calcutta, armed them with guns to protect his property and the European staff at the mill. No threats to property or people at Rishra materialised.

The jute mill at Rishra was a very important development for the jute industry. For it was the first of several that were built in Calcutta, most of which were managed and maintained by Dundonians who became known as jutewallahs. Over time, the jute industry in Calcutta boomed and eventually displaced the Dundee jute industry because it produced jute more cheaply and efficiently.

David had returned to Dundee by 1861 and lived in Scouring Burn, the district where many employees of the textile industry lived and the location of many textile mills and factories. David remained a mechanic in the textile industry throughout his life and most of his children followed him into the industry. As a textile mechanic in Dundee, David was not short of potential employers because there were so many mills and factories. In 1861 there were seventy three spinning mills and weaving factories in Dundee and an even greater number of jute employers. David died aged sixty eight in 1888. His widow, Mary Andrews died aged seventy six in 1900.

David Ferguson (the fourth)

David Ferguson (the fourth), was born in1851, in Dundee. Children in Dundee were then educated to the age of about thirteen in one of the fourteen parochial schools. In the 1860s, a third of all children in Scotland attended no schools, especially in the industrial areas and sizeable proportion of the rest had no more than a year or two of instruction. David followed his father's occupation and became a mechanic. In 1874, he married Margaret Brown, in the United Presbyterian Church which had seceded from the established Church of Scotland. They became the parents of five children in eleven years, two of whom did not survive infancy.

Margaret Brown, like her sister, was a power loom weaver in the jute industry. The industry produced many items such as sacking, carpets, sandbags, sailcloth, and tents. In their employment, the sisters were typical female Dundonians. It has been estimated that at its peak, the textile industry in Dundee at the end of the 1800s employed almost fifty thousand people or half the working population. Women jute workers outnumbered men by three to one. However, wages in Dundee were possibly the lowest in Scotland, although the cost of living was highest. In contrast, the owners of the jute industry, the jute barons, grew fabulously wealthy and chose to leave the grime and dirt of Dundee to build their mansions in Broughty Ferry, where there was clean healthy air. David Ferguson was employed in the jute industry during its period of greatest expansion (1870 – 1890) when the industry was at its peak. As a mechanic and later an engineer, he was highly skilled and well paid, unlike those in other occupations in the industry.

From being a jute mechanic in Dundee, David, like his father, became a jutewallah in Calcutta. He was one of the three thousand Dundonians employed in the jute industry in Calcutta, India at the end of the 1800s. He and his family were in Calcutta from 1879 to 1884. In 1882 he was manager of the Balliaghata Jute Mill, built in 1875, and his employer was the Barnagore Jute Manufacturing Company.

In starting and finishing as a jutewallah, David and his family enjoyed the exciting experience of a long journey by boat between Scotland and India. The journey made by David, his wife Margaret and their first child, from Dundee to Calcutta was by jute clipper. Jute clippers were sailing ships which were built for speed. There were fifteen vessels in the fleet of the Dundee Clipper Line, most of which were built in Dundee. The Lochee made the fastest ever run under sail, from Calcutta to Dundee in only 90 days, in 1882. Many clippers carried emigrants to Australia and New Zealand, so Calcutta was not the final destination. Typical of the jute clippers was the Camperdown, built in 1875, celebrated as a rapid carrier of cargo as well as being equipped to carry almost five hundred passengers. The journey and return made by David and family was round the Cape of Good Hope. Clippers could not use the Suez Canal which had been completed in 1869 but steam ships could and before long they cut the length of journeys to the East by their greater efficiency and rendered the clipper trade route as obsolete.

In becoming a jutewallah, David had succeeded in a very competitive field. For at this time there were ten good applicants for every jutewallah vacancy in Calcutta. His appointment therefore was the result of him having demonstrated sufficient expertise and motivation. The jutewallahs were employed both to install the equipment and machinery in the mills and to provide the maintenance and supervision in this expanding industry. In the 1900s, Calcutta eventually overtook Dundee and displaced it from its premier place in world jute manufacturing. Many Dundonians who were employed in jute manufacturing in Calcutta stayed for many years before returning home. Few remained there.

David lived in India for only a few years. The prospect of good earnings and a high standard of living was the attraction for many and the rewards were sufficiently strong to keep them in India for many years (sustained by regular spells of home leave). Although they worked hard for long hours in a climate that was difficult for them, the life of the jutewallah was one of privilege and comfort. The financial rewards of working in Calcutta were immense. A jutewallah would live rent free in a company house and have a bearer to attend to personal and household needs. There would be annual pay increases and bonuses.

The return of David and Margaret to Dundee after only a few years was prompted by their concern for their children. One child had died in Dundee before they left for India and one child born in Calcutta had not survived. Margaret became pregnant again in 1884 and she and David were fearful of the risks to their unborn child if they remained in Calcutta. They wished to avoid another tragedy occurring in Calcutta and decided to return to Dundee to safeguard the life of their expected child. Their fourth and fifth children were born respectively in 1885 and 1886, in Dundee.

On his return to Dundee, David continued his employment in the jute industry, initially employed as a mechanic but later as a self-employed engineer with his own business. His experience as a manager in Calcutta, may have given him the know-how and taste for being his own boss. He acquired premises for a machine shop where he devised new machinery that he could sell to jute manufacturers. Although he owned his business premises he did not own the house that the family lived in, preferring to rent, as was the custom of the day. Having lived at the same address for about eight years, the family's address then changed three times in rapid succession between 1894 and 1896.

David Ferguson died prematurely at home aged forty four in 1896. Alcoholism was the cause of his early death. The rapid changes of address in the last two years of his life may have indicated the chaos besetting David as a result of his alcoholism. Alcohol abuse was an extensive problem in Dundee in David's lifetime and after and it was also an illness that affected other members of the Ferguson family. It was not by mere chance that the city elected in 1922, a Member of Parliament who was committed to the prohibition of alcohol. He is the only person ever elected to the House of Commons on a prohibitionist policy.

The financial loss to David's family from his death was immediate. There was no money for them and because he had not made a will, it was necessary for his widow, Margaret, to use the Dundee Sheriff Court to secure access to his estate. The estate amounted to £43 3s and 10p. Household furniture and other effects were valued at £10 10s whilst the remainder of the estate was of the value of £32 13s 10p. The remainder was the sum of an unpaid balance for items sold and delivered to a customer by David, prior to his death. The machine shop business premises only had an annual rental value of twelve pounds. The meagre financial provision for Margaret on the death of her husband suggests that David's alcoholism eroded his professional accomplishments and reduced him to penury.

David's premature death was a devastating loss to the family. However, it did not stop his son Harry, from pursuing a career inspired by his father and grandfather. Following his apprenticeship, training at Dundee Technical College and employment as a mechanic in the jute industry, Harry found work in South Africa as a mechanic in a gold mine initially, before fulfilling his aspiration in 1912 of becoming a manager of a jute mill in Calcutta. In 1922, he married in India and then returned to Dundee in 1925 for retirement. In his retirement, he built miniature railway engines.

In the aftermath of David's death, Margaret faced a difficult time as a widow when she had to support her family of three without a breadwinner. The two youngest children were aged eleven and nine and the eldest, a jute weaver, was the source of household income. Margaret did not return to employment in the jute industry. The prospect was unattractive given that work for most women involved drudgery, exhaustion, low wages and constant danger. Margaret contributed to the family income by being a mangle keeper. In this role she charged housewives for the use of her wringer to press linen and cloth. She was a tenant of one of the houses her builder father owned and let. Her straitened circumstances suggest that it was let rent-free. Her father may have given her other financial support. Within a few years, all three of Margaret's children had incomes from their work in the jute industry. After the death of her mother in 1906, Margaret, her children and father formed a household that occupied two of the houses her father owned. For a time, Margaret's sister and family were neighbours and tenants in another of the houses owned by her father. Margaret looked after her father until his death in 1917. In her later years, Margaret lived with her daughter Eva and family in a house rented by the local authority. She died in 1937.

Eva Ferguson

Eva Mary Ferguson was born in 1886. Her childhood years fell under the shadow of her father's alcoholism and his premature death when she was aged ten. She changed primary schools in Dundee at least twice, perhaps an outcome of the chaos caused by her father's alcoholism. The impact of her home circumstances on her schooling could only have been detrimental to some extent. However, for other Dundee children, schooling was limited as a result of it being part-time. The Dundee School Board was notorious for allowing children to work for six hours a day if they attended school for the other half day. In 1896, two thousand seven hundred and ninety three children under the age of fourteen were employed in Dundee mills. Dundee was a city dominated by and reliant on the jute industry and the acceptance of part-time schooling was only abolished in 1918.

After leaving school, Eva found employment at a dye works, initially as a clerk and later as a packer. A memorable event in her youth was her admission to Buffalo Bill's Wild West show when it visited Dundee in August 1904. On its tours in Britain, the show was enjoyed by nobility, commoners and Queen Victoria herself. In 1914, Eva married Thomas Sinclair Maxwell Drever. After marriage, Eva eschewed paid work to shoulder responsibility for domestic tasks and child rearing. She and Thomas had three children in twelve years. The rest of Eva's life with Thomas is described in chapter 11.

Chapter 11

Auks

In the Orkney Isles, the inhabitants of each district had their own nickname although they are largely forgotten today. An inhabitant of the island of Westray in Orkney was known as an auk. It is a dialect term for the common guillemot which is particular to the island. The paternal forebears of Thomas Sinclair Maxwell Drever were inhabitants of Westray and so were auks. The story of these paternal forebears starts in1492, with the origins of the surname Drever in the Northern Isles, a place of Norse settlement. The Drevers were peasants who farmed and fished in the Orkney Isles, for hundreds of years and may have had a bloodline from shipwrecked Spanish sailors.

In this chapter, the lives of seven Drever forbears are profiled in direct order of descent starting with John in mid-1700s. John's son, Thomas lived when many peasants made kelp as a side-line. Thomas's son, another John, rented enough acres of land to require the hire of labour, which made him a farmer. His son, another Thomas, combined commercial fishing with small scale farming. Thomas's son, James, married a farmer's daughter and succeeded to her father's farm tenancy. James's son, Charles, a ploughman, left Westray for the Orkney island of Sanday and then eschewed rural Orkney for urban life in Dundee. Charles's son, Thomas, lived mainly in Dundee, where he was a machineman for a local newspaper, a WW1 conscript and a Presbyterian stalwart.

Origins of the Drevers

Surnames were first used permanently in Orkney in the 1300s. According to one authoritative source, the Drever surname in Scotland was confined to Orkney and Shetland and it first appeared in records when Brandy Dravar and John Dravar gave evidence in 1492 on how the butter stent (or tax) was paid. The taxes were paid to the Earl of Orkney by the inhabitants of the islands, most of who were descended from Norse settlers. Therefore, the Drever family, were descended from the Norse or Viking settlers who first occupied Orkney from 800 A D. Recent DNA research confirms that a high proportion of the present inhabitants of Orkney have Norse origins. The descendants of the Norse settlers who came to inhabit Orkney only came under Scottish rule in 1468.

Orkney from the time of Norse settlement was a farming community and so it seems, the Drevers were peasant farmers for hundreds of years. The population broadly comprised large landowners, who were the nobility and peasants who were either cottars or udallers. The cottars were a large labour force of serfs who were subservient to their masters and were paid with scraps of land, rather than money, in return for never ending and ill-defined personal services. The udallers, who were smaller in number, were peasants, too but were independent owner occupiers. Therefore, the peasants were broadly of two different kinds, with one more dependent on the land owning nobility than the other. Available evidence suggests that the the Drevers from the earliest of times were peasants who owned no land.

Many of the peasants lived in townships in multiple occupancy of variable size, sometimes with twenty households or more. Instead of square fields, the arable land lay typically in a bewildering strip patchwork of hundreds of corn rigs, yellow with charlock and purple with valerian, intermixed with sections of rough grassland on which animals might be tethered in summer. The run-rig system was based on the principles of sharing land and rotating between tenants. It was different from the system of the same name that prevailed elsewhere in Scotland by being more complex. The complexity arose from property being defined in terms of a share rather than a fixed boundary and the land allocated to tenants was not in simple fractions. Each township managed poorer-quality hill ground as common grazing for cattle and sheep. Pasture was common property.

Besides farming, fishing for home consumption was common amongst the Orkney population from the earliest of times. Shellfish were caught in prehistoric times and the Vikings made catches of herring, cod and ling. The Vikings organised the settlement of Orkney in such a way that the basic needs were observed for access to the sea, land for crops and grazing for animals. As a result, the Orcadians developed considerable boating skills that like their farming skills, were passed on to succeeding generations

The agricultural system of Orkney and the way of life that accompanied it remained largely the same for several hundred years. Five hundred years of Norse settlement laid a basic structure for the way of life to which there was an overlay of Scottish culture over several hundred years. When significant changes occurred in agriculture, (starting in the 1700s), they were later in the Orkney Isles than for the rest of Britain. One interesting development occurred on Westray prior to surviving records and may have included Drever forebears.

The Westray Dons

In addition to their Norse ancestry, the Drevers may have been partly descended from Spaniards, the Spanish bloodline having been acquired from the 1600s. A legend has persisted that as a result of a ship wreck from the Spanish Armada in 1588, a small number of Spanish seamen made a landing in Westray, where they settled, being accepted by the local people. They married local girls and took their surnames, their own being unpronounceable. The families they founded went by the names, Balfour and Hewison and in time the names Petrie, Reid, Rendall and Logie were added. The families of the Spanish seamen and their descendants were known as the Dons of Westray. At first they were distinct in appearance for their Mediterranean physical features marked them out from the rest of the inhabitants and they also kept to themselves, not permitting marriage outside their own circle but before long they ceased to be a separate group in the local population.

Whilst the legend is unproven it has been considered sufficiently credible for a leading geneticist to investigate it in a DNA research programme of the population in Scotland. No result to confirm the legend may ever emerge however, because in general, the genetic inheritance of the Orcadians and the Spanish is not significantly different. If the legend is true, it is possible that the Drevers may have shared the ancestry of the Spanish sailors who integrated with the Westray population. Inter-marriage between those connected to the Westray Dons and the Drevers could have occurred in the 1600s and 1700s.

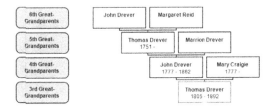

The 'first' Drever

The 'first' ancestor of Thomas Sinclair Maxwell to appear in the church registers for Westray, was John Drever. He and Margaret Reid (was she descended from the Westray Dons?) were the parents of two sons and four daughters between 1746 and 1764. However, because the church registers for Westray before 1731 have not survived and there are significant gaps in the records after 1731, little is known specifically about the lives of John Drever and Margaret Reid.

The gaps in the church records for Westray are matched by gaps in records of the church courts (Kirk Sessions). For although there was a church on Westray as early as 1137, Kirk Session minutes have only survived from 1835. So another important source that might have revealed titbits about the Drevers is largely silent. Nonetheless, from historical evidence of Orkney, an understanding of the life of John and Margaret can be obtained.

The peasantry cultivated crops on their own little bit of land, grazed sheep and cattle on the less fertile common land and performed much the same tasks on behalf of a tenant farmer or landowner: turning out to fetch and carry when required to and to plough, sow, and harvest, cut peat, carry up seaweed to manure the land and to labour in the barn. The Orcadian peasants also used their boating skills for fishing to help feed their families. Boating skills also made travel possible for sea transport was the commonest method of travel.

Roads were almost non-existent in Westray during the 1700s when carts were first introduced to the island. There was no regular shipping service and in 1755 the population of the island was almost thirteen hundred. It was the boating skills of Orcadian men after 1740 that led to their employment in high numbers by the Hudson's Bay Company, whose business was fur trading. The incomplete records of the company do not indicate that John was employed, nor were his descendants apparently. Instead, John may have used his boating skills, as many of his peers did, for smuggling, a common pastime in Orkney it seems.

One important economic development occurred during John's life that differentiated it in one respect, from the lives of his predecessors. Beginning in Orkney in 1720, kelp making boomed and was central to the islands economy between 1760 and 1820. Kelp was collected and processed for alkali and later for iodine until the industry ended in the 1930s. During the boom years kelp-making employed thousands of families. They were employed in harvesting a huge quantity of seaweed. The seaweed was cut, collected and dried. It was then burnt in a kelp kiln and turned into a hard coarse substance which was shipped to ports around Britain where it was mainly used by glass manufacturers, soap-makers and dye-makers. Kelp-making was not popular with those engaged in it, for it was arduous, unpleasant and ill-paid work. It could be obligatory work for peasants who held land from landowners and it also provided them with some much needed income, particularly when harvests were poor. Did John Drever and his family make kelp? The answer has to be very probably, given the historical evidence. It is also very probable that his successors did this work too.

Thomas Drever

Thomas, the eldest son of John, was born in 1751. He married Marrion Drever, whose maiden name suggests that she may have been a relative. Between 1774 and 1787, Thomas and Marrion had one son and four daughters.

Thomas was a peasant of modest resources and therefore not one of the sixteen tenant farmers on Westray with a liability to pay the farm horse tax in 1793. After 1750, change started to occur in farming in Orkney and the period has been described as an age of agricultural improvement. The changes were various but principal amongst them were the break-up of large estates and the displacement of many peasants. Some of them became crofters. Crofts were created from the reclamation of common land and land that was uncultivated, which was substantial at this time. Typically, a croft was about five acres and a crofter followed a particular way of life which combined farming, with labour for the landowner or other farmers. A crofter rented his small land holding and a croft was too small to necessitate the hire of labour. A crofter was likely to keep a pig, a cow, and some poultry. Oats and potatoes were commonly grown by crofters with no green crops like hay or turnips.

Crofters also fished a little and made kelp. Westray is ten miles long and between half a mile to six and a quarter miles broad so its inhabitants had a relatively short distance to travel to the coast. In 1793, fishing was prevalent amongst the Westray population of sixteen hundred and twenty nine, with eighty two boats used for that purpose. Coalfish and dogfish were amongst the fish that were caught, although fishing was a side line. Boats were used for transportation and at this time no one in the parish earned their living from fishing.

The domestic economic activities of crofters' households suggest what Marrion Drever and her four daughters did. The females in such households were busy spinning flax (which was imported into Orkney), weaving linen and straw plaiting. Straw plaiting produced items such as baskets, hats and bonnets. The women were also engaged in turning wool into clothing. Because spinning, weaving and straw plaiting continued to be commonplace in the 1800s in Orkney, female Drever successors most probably engaged in this work too.

John Drever

John Drever, the only son of Thomas, was born in 1777 on Westray. He married Mary Craigie and they had four sons between 1805 and 1817. In the early part of John's life between 1793 and 1815, Britain was at war with France and a large number of the male population were mobilised for military service. Because of their boating skills, many Orcadian men were either press ganged or volunteered for the Royal Navy. Otherwise, they served in the militia. However, there appears to be no record of John Drever in either branch of military service. So there is a mystery about his early life during the French revolutionary and Napoleonic wars.

John lived at a time when the pace of change in agriculture in the Orkney Isles was quickening and crofting proliferated. By 1841, he was in possession of some land at Langskaill and by 1851 he was a farmer with forty nine acres who employed two labourers. The land was rented for £7 7s annually from John Stewart, a member of a noble land-owning family. It appears that John probably started as a crofter (and part-time kelp maker) and extended his landholding over the years. Later in his life he became a tenant farmer, whose farm albeit small, was big enough to require hired labour. Neighbouring properties to John's farm were occupied by John's sons and their families which suggests that they all helped one another. John had become a widower by 1841, when his household comprised a domestic servant, Margaret Smith and two grandsons aged fifteen and nine. By 1861, John's farm was thirty acres and he had relinquished the tenancy to his son Samuel. He died at Langskaill, Westray, in 1862, aged eighty four.

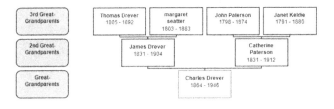

Thomas Drever

Thomas Drever, the eldest son of John, was born in 1805 on Westray and he married Margaret Seatter in 1825. They had four sons and five daughters between 1826 and 1847.

Thomas was one of the many Orcadians with the surname Drever in the 1800s, for Censuses show the name as the tenth most common surname in the Orkney Islands and more frequent in Westray than any other island. Thomas farmed and fished at Langskaill for much of his working life. Like his father, he probably started as a crofter who expanded his landholding to eleven acres by 1851 and to nineteen acres by 1871. His landholding became large enough to warrant the employment of one labourer. Although kelp making declined after 1830, it did not cease until the 1930s, so this activity was still undertaken by many peasants in Orkney like Thomas.

In his fishing, Thomas collaborated with his son Thomas and his brother John. They were very typical of the agrarian population of Orkney in pursuing two separate but complementary economic activities to offset the risks that were acute at the time from reliance on just one activity. Because both fishing and farming were seasonal in nature, the trick for Westray men like Thomas who did both, was to attend to the different activities at the right times.

Commercial fishing in Westray started in the 1800s and the fishing grounds around the island were plentiful. Lobster, herring, pollock and haddock were caught. Thomas's ancestors had engaged in fishing as a subsistence activity but for him, fishing became a business which yielded income. Both line and nets were used and the island had seven or eight small craft and thirty large herring boats with nets in 1841. Storage and other facilities were developed at Pierowall Bay so that fish could be caught and sold for the market outside Westray. Processes were developed for drying, filleting, gutting, salting and icing the fish prior to being shipped south. These processes provided employment for the women of Westray, amongst who were Thomas's wife and his five daughters. He and his family may have participated in whale hunting when it was a domestic exercise of a sporadic nature and still conducted in the 1860s. The whales were driven ashore and slaughtered, principally for food and oil.

Thomas was illiterate, shown by his mark, instead of a signature on the registration of his wife's death in 1883. In 1841, there were fifty two, older people on Westray who were illiterate, out of a population of two thousand. In Thomas's childhood, there was very little or no schooling on the island so his illiteracy was probably a result.

Thomas had retired from farming by 1881 and he died aged eighty five in 1893.

James Drever

James Drever, the second eldest son of Thomas, was born in 1831 on Westray. He married Catherine Paterson and they had nine boys between 1855 and 1871.

The Westray of James's early years was in a rudimentary state. Improvement that had occurred in agriculture had been on a very limited scale and it appears that Westray had lagged behind the other Orkney islands in its ways. The farm-houses were described at the time as miserable hovels and had been built by poor tenants themselves (rather than the landowners). There were cattle at one end and people at the other end and there was mingling between the two. Most of the island's inhabitants only scraped a bare livelihood. Of the eight families who owned land on Westray, only two were resident on the island.

The population of two thousand was dispersed around Westray, and the only semblance to a village was at Pierowall, which consisted of about a dozen houses. There were no highways, no proper harbour, and no regular communications with Kirkwall which was twenty miles away and the nearest market town. There was no system of regular mail delivery. Westray's cultural distance from the rest of the country was, illustrated by the old Julian calendar being followed in 1866, with a celebration of New Year on 13 January. The Julian calendar had been abandoned for the Gregorian calendar officially by Britain in 1752 but the people of Westray kept to the old way.

Some changes did occur in Westray during James's life: in 1836, the institution of a regular paddle steamer service followed by regular mail delivery; in 1845 a hospital was opened; in 1848, Government assistance for drainage and improvement of property through long-term loans. By 1841 there were four schools serving the island and there was no longer illiteracy amongst children of school age.

James left home in his teens and by 1851 was employed as labourer by John Paterson, at his farm at Cotohowan, Westray.

James courted and married Catherine, his employer's daughter. She was an only child. After their marriage they remained members of the Paterson household and they raised their nine boys on the farm at Cotohowan. In 1871, the farm amounted to twenty five acres, fifteen of which were arable. James Drever's sons provided the farm with a labour force until they left home. Farming was combined with fishing at Cotohowan, where James's son, Thomas, was a fisherman. James's employer and father-in-law, John Paterson, rented the farm for £10 annually from the Earl of Zetland. When John died aged seventy six in 1874, the tenancy of the farm passed to James. John's widow, Jessie Paterson, remained in her son-in-law's household until her death, aged eighty six in 1880.

On James's death aged seventy three in 1904, the tenancy of the farm at Cotohowan passed to his son, Thomas. James's widow, Catherine, remained in Thomas's household until her death at eighty one years in 1912. Thomas Drever fished and farmed at Cotohowan until his death in 1935.

Charles Drever

Charles Drever, the fifth eldest son of James, was born in 1864 at the family farm, Cotohowan, Westray. He married Ann Scott Peace in 1884 and they had nine children in nineteen years. They left Orkney in 1898 and settled in Dundee.

Charles left the family farm in his teens. At the age of sixteen, in 1881, he was one of the four young farm servants employed by Robert Rendall at Noltland Dykeside farm on Westray. Before long, he followed in the tracks of his eldest brother John by leaving Westray for the island of Sanday, Orkney. John, an agricultural labourer, had married a Sanday girl, Isabella Peace in 1878. Charles may have learned from his brother, that Sanday, with a more flourishing agricultural economy than Westray, offered better opportunities for being hired as a farm hand. Charles soon obtained work and met his future wife. She was Ann Scott Peace who was a year older than him, a domestic servant, and the sister of Isabella, who had married his oldest brother, John. Her father was a farmer and master mason. Charles and Ann were married in 1884, in the dissenting United Presbyterian church on the island, when he was aged twenty. After their marriage, Charles and Ann had six children whilst they lived on Sanday.

In 1885, Charles and his brother John were employed by a retired military officer, Major George Howard. They were two of the four ploughmen that he employed and housed. As a married man on Sanday, Charles had three different employers over fourteen years. As a ploughman, Charles's activities were wider than ploughing alone, which was only seasonal. The job of ploughman was also known as horseman. For the job entailed responsibility for feeding the animals, harnessing them for ploughs and pulling wagons and carts as well as checking the condition of their shoes, knowing about their health and tending them when sick if a vet was not available.

The houses that Charles and his family inhabited on Sanday did not have a rateable or rental value which suggests that they were elementary in their facilities. Charles was listed in the records as an inhabitant of a property in 1885 and 1895, not a tenant, occupier or proprietor. A more detailed picture of the houses inhabited by Charles on Sanday is suggested by an official report on agricultural labourers. The report published in 1893 included the Orkney islands. The cottages were frequently without ventilation and unsatisfactory from dampness. They were 'rude in construction', with stone and lime walls, one room, fifteen foot by twelve foot, with a closet, nine foot by eight foot, leading off. The room may have had a fireplace. There were no pantries or cupboards and no exterior convenience. There was no drainage and the water supply was a well, at some distance from the house. The historical evidence suggests that Charles's housing was minimal in its condition and facilities. His housing was part-payment of his total wage as a labourer. In 1895, the proprietor of his house was his employer, the Marquis of Zetland.

The official report in 1893 suggests that Charles worked an eleven to twelve hour day, starting at 5 a.m. with fewer hours only on Sunday. Holidays amounted to three of four days a year. The annual average total wage in Orkney in 1893 for a labourer was £34 to £37, of which £15 was in money, the rest comprising payment in kind, for example, potatoes milk and shelter. Whilst Charles lived on Orkney, there was plenty of work for him, partly because mechanisation had not yet been introduced into farming there. As a labourer on Orkney, Charles had regularity of employment, certainty of wages and hours, accommodation for many months, a short distance to work, and a full wage during sickness. Despite these benefits from his work, Charles and Ann and their six children left Sanday for Dundee in 1898. Why did he leave?

For many peasants in Orkney after 1800, the prospect of a better life had been secured through the possession of several acres of land as a crofter. Many peasants had been able to improve their lot through acquiring and developing bits of common land and uncultivated land. Charles's ancestors, John and Thomas, appeared to have done just that. But changes in the use and enclosure of land had massively reduced the possibilities of becoming a crofter by the end of the 1800s. Therefore, Charles may have recognised that a better life for him and family was not a realistic prospect in Orkney.

When Charles migrated from Orkney to Dundee, he followed in the footsteps of many Orcadians who had migrated to the Empire (as it then was), or to mainland Scotland after 1850. There was massive net out-migration from Orkney which contributed to a fall in population from thirty one thousand in 1851 to twenty five thousand in 1911. The movement of population from the country to the towns for better opportunities, particularly higher wages, was also widespread throughout Scotland in this period. More specific incentives for migration arose for Orcadians, from 1880, when prices of grain and cattle experienced a downturn in the islands; prosperity declined and a lasting period of stagnation and depression began. Orkney was an agrarian economy with few opportunities compared to mainland Scotland. Charles decided that migration would secure a better future for his children.

An important influence on the decision of Charles to migrate may have been the example of three of his brothers. Older brother, Peter, an agricultural labourer, had migrated to Aberdeenshire by 1881 when he was aged of twenty one. He married in 1889 and remained in agricultural employment in Aberdeenshire for the rest of his working life, dying in 1949 in Aberdeen. Younger brother, George, was an agricultural labourer when he joined the Seaforth Highlanders at Fort George on the Moray Firth in 1886. He remained on the Moray Firth where he married in 1891 and was promoted to sergeant. After leaving the forces he moved to Glasgow and became a doorkeeper. He re-enlisted in the Seaforth Highlanders in 1914 for one year and was an acting company sergeant major when he was discharged in 1915. He was awarded two campaign medals for his WW1 service and received an army pension. He died in Glasgow in 1924. Younger brother, Alexander, became an ordinary seaman and in 1891, his ship with a crew of one hundred of mixed nationality, was berthed at Bo'ness, West Lothian. Soon after, he became a dock labourer in Leith, where he married in 1896 and lived there for the rest of his life.

By migrating to Dundee and other destinations on the east coast, the Drever brothers were following a customary path for migrants from the Northern Isles. Travel from Orkney was by boat and the sea routes were to Scotland's east coast. Migrants from the Hebrides usually had Glasgow as their destination, for that is where the sea routes took them. In choosing Dundee as his destination, Charles may have known from his brother Alexander, at Leith, that the city waterfront offered possibilities for employment. In any event, as a migrant to mainland Scotland, the waterfront of a city may have been an obvious place to seek work. Certainly during the 1800s, Irish emigrants were heavily represented in dock labour in Scotland.

When he arrived in Dundee seeking work, Charles was an unskilled man of thirty three years. However, as a labourer, he could offer strength and muscle, suitable qualities for the Dundee Harbour Board to hire him as a labourer in 1898 until his retirement. In arriving in Dundee in 1898, Charles came to a city that was economically successful and of rising importance. According to the *Dundee Directory 1897-8*, trade had been good, there was plenty of work for willing hands and the city was prosperous. In Dundee, three more children were born to Charles and Ann between 1899 and 1904, one of whom did not survive childhood.

Charles was one of forty three men employed as labourers by Dundee Harbour Board. They were the largest occupational group in the labour force of two hundred and forty men in a variety of trades. The labourers employed by the Harbour Board were separate from the dock labourers and stevedores (one thousand and sixty nine strong in 1907) who were employed by shipping companies and shipping brokers. In 1907, his weekly pay was £1 10s 0p which was the average pay for the labourers employed by the Board. In the Board's workforce, some occupations earned more, for example, the blacksmiths (£1 15s 11p) and some earned less, for example, the scavengers (£1 3s 6p). The administrative staffs, of course, were generally paid more than the manual workers.

Charles's specific job was harbour stoker. He stoked fresh coal into the furnaces of boilers on coal-powered steam engines for the operation of heavy machinery in the form of cranes, harbour gates and swing bridges. Steam engines were distributed all around the quays and one crane introduced in 1873, was sixty tons. The cranes were needed for lifting cargoes in and out of ships' holds. Jute, flax, hemp, coal, and timber were major imports, whilst linen, jute manufactures and yarns were major exports. Steam power at the harbour was gradually supplemented by hydraulic systems (moveable jigger hoists) and later by electricity (travelling cranes) and these methods eventually replaced steam power completely. Charles's job as a stoker therefore became obsolete, but not it seems before he reached retirement. He reached sixty five years in 1929.

If Charles expected to get a better life by migrating to Dundee, he succeeded; it is evident that he secured an improved standard of living in his housing and income. The family's first house in Dundee, 131 Rosebank Street, had an annual rental value of £9 9s. Households in Dundee living in houses with an annual rental value of £5 or under were considered to be poor, by the Poor Law authorities. The property that Charles tenanted was not of a low rental value unlike the houses he had inhabited on Sanday, which had no rental value and correspondingly limited facilities and conditions. In Dundee in 1907, Charles's total annual wage was about £78 in contrast to his total annual wage on Sanday which was between £34 and £37. Not only was his wage in Dundee much better than on Sanday, it was very good for a man in his occupation. For the annual average wage of a general labourer in 1911 in the UK was £74, with the annual average for Scotland being a few pounds less than that. Furthermore, historical sources suggest that his occupation in Dundee brought him shorter hours and longer holidays than on Orkney and regular secure work for the rest of his life. He encountered losses of course. The most obvious was the surrender of a spacious natural environment for a congested urban one. It is easy to imagine that he had to make a big adjustment from ploughing the fields and other varied tasks on a small, lightly populated, agrarian island to shovelling coal into a furnace all day on a big city waterfront.

Charles seems to have possessed a considerable physical stamina for he remained a stoker until his retirement. He may have been lucky also to have escaped serious accidents which could occur at the Harbour. Should he have encountered a mishap at work, he might have been assisted by his employer, for it had a discretionary power from 1911, to give financial support to employees who had become disabled, or after long service, were unable to continue.

This provision suggests that Dundee Harbour Board was in general, a considerate employer, of whom Charles was a beneficiary. The Board was a publicly accountable body, with its members appointed as representative of a wide range of local interests.

In his Dundee habitat, Charles seems to have kept in touch with family in Westray, hence the inclusion of a lodger in his household in 1901. John Thomson, a single, Westray born man, aged twenty one, was a Tramways labourer. It is possible that the lodger was a distant relative, for Charles's brother Thomas, had married into a Thomson family in Westray.

Charles Drever became a widower in 1924. Subsequently, in 1933 he was re-married to Elspeth Crawford, a jute weaver and in his retirement he and Elspeth moved from the centre of Dundee to the suburb of Monifieth, where he died in 1946, aged eighty two.

Thomas Sinclair Maxwell Drever

Thomas Sinclair Maxwell Drever, the eldest son of Charles Drever, was born on Sanday in 1888. He married Eva Mary Ferguson and they had three children between 1915 and 1927,

Thomas left Sanday for Dundee when he was aged ten. He retained affectionate memories of his birthplace, particularly of the beaches as a natural playground, but he never returned. In 1902, when the second Boer war in South Africa had ended and he was fourteen years, he left school for work and in 1904 he was employed by John Leng & Co Ltd. where he became a machineman on the local newspaper, the Dundee Advertiser. Thomas's employment mirrored that of a relative, George Scott whose family had left Sanday for Dundee around 1894. It suggests that his relative may have helped him to obtain his job. In the newspaper industry, the machinemen possessed less skill than other trades, for which an apprenticeship of several years had to be served. In starting his job, Thomas had to get used to the noise of the printing presses in action and the risks of the work. As a result of an accident, his right hand was scarred on the first and second fingers. In 1905, John Leng & Co Ltd merged with Thomson, the other major publisher in Dundee, under the leadership of D.C. Thomson.

In 1914, Thomas married Eva Mary Ferguson and the first of their three children, Doris was born in 1915. World War One had commenced in 1914 and Thomas's two single, younger brothers, James and John, enlisted into the army. Aged twenty nine in February 1918, Thomas was conscripted into the Royal Garrison Artillery, at the Citadel, Plymouth. He was given the rank of gunner and was then in training for the next few months. The Royal Garrison Artillery developed from fortress-based artillery located on British coasts. From 1914 when the army possessed very little heavy artillery, it grew into a very large component of the British forces. It was armed with heavy, large calibre guns and howitzers that were positioned some way behind the front line and had immense destructive power. The Royal Garrison Artillery, the Royal Horse Artillery and the Royal Field Artillery formed the Royal Artillery. In 1918, the strength of the Royal Artillery in France was five hundred and forty eight thousand, seven hundred and eighty officers and men.

Thomas joined the 544th Siege Battery, 11th Heavy Artillery Group (or Brigade), in Flanders, in July 1918. His Brigade, part of the Fifth Army, was constituted by five siege batteries and had been on the Western Front since January 1918. The siege battery was a basic unit in the Royal Garrison Artillery. It numbered about six officers and ninety other ranks in 1918. The siege batteries were most often employed in destroying or neutralising the enemy artillery, as well as putting destructive fire down on strongpoints, dumps, store, roads and railways behind enemy lines. The purpose was to allow British infantry and tanks to advance at much reduced risk. The battery personnel lived and sheltered in dugouts and they took cover from their armaments when their position was under bombardment. They had to get used to the terrific noise and flashes of light from the activity of their own and the enemy artillery. When they were under bombardment, the sights and sounds were terrifying. However, even in the more active parts of the front, battle was rarely continuous and boredom was common.

The armaments of the 11th HAG were 6-inch, 9.2-inch and 12-inch howitzers. The 6-inch howitzer fired shells that weighed one hundred pound at a maximum range of seven thousand yards. The 9.2-inch howitzers fired shells of that weighed two hundred and ninety pounds at a maximum range of thirteen thousand, nine hundred and thirty five yards and the 12-inch howitzers fired shells that weighed seven hundred and fifty pounds at a maximum range of fifteen thousand yards. Howitzers were short barrelled and fired upwards so they sent large calibre high explosive shells in high trajectory and plunging fire. The howitzers could not be moved easily or quickly and were transported by open topped and open fronted gun carriers on tracks. The very large howitzers were railway mounted. Usually, four small or two large howitzers were operated by a siege battery with a crew of between eight and twelve men for each weapon. Each howitzer was carefully camouflaged from aerial observation.

The 11th HAG conducted regular shelling of the enemy in July and August. In a typical day, 11th HAG neutralized several active hostile batteries and carried out harassing fire on suitable targets. These targets included Laventie station, La Gorgue station, Pont Riqueul, Estaires and various crossroads and ammunition dumps. The targeting of the shelling was reliant on observation by spotter aircraft or tethered balloons or by ground level observation. Later on, as the Fifth Army advanced, new targets were identified, for example, Aubers and Fromelles.

The 11th HAG was subject to frequent shelling from long range enemy guns, day and night. It varied from normal, to above normal to below normal. Whatever damage the enemy guns inflicted, they did not successfully target the batteries of 11th HAG in the summer of 1918, according to the war diary. In contrast, during the German offensive in Spring1918, the enemy long range guns damaged the batteries and caused casualties. Even when damage was not inflicted, the effect of frequent shelling on the battery personnel by distant enemy artillery can be imagined.

On the 20th July the 544th Siege Battery carried out harassing fire with aeroplane observation on an ammunition dump, with twenty seven rounds being fired by the Battery. Two explosions were caused and the flames of one fire were a hundred feet high. On the 11th August, the Battery, with balloon observation, carried out a neutralization of active enemy railway guns. Eight rounds were fired and three hits on the railway were obtained. On 18th August, the Battery with ground observation fired some ranging shots on two ammunition dumps.

The 11th HAG continued shelling the enemy during September to assist the Allied advance in Flanders. In the following month, there was some shelling of the enemy up to October 13th but none after. During the month, the Brigade HQ moved to La Gorgue and all available personnel were engaged in railway repair and reconstruction at various centres connected with lines to Bethune, Lille, Armentieres and La Gorgue. This work was probably undertaken to enable movement of the railway mounted howitzers to new destinations. If there was a spell of boredom for 11th HAG, it may have occurred in the latter part of October, when bombardment and counter-bombardment had ceased. In November, personnel had returned from their railway repair work. Therefore, well before the official termination of hostilities on the 11th November, 1918, the howitzers of the 11th HAG had fallen silent.

The military campaigns in which Thomas served were the advance in Flanders and the final advance in Artois. In Flanders, between the 18 August and 6 September, the Fifth and Second Armies began operations in the Lys valley and recaptured miles of ground that had been lost earlier in the year. Between 2 October and 11 November, the First and Fifth Armies liberated the French coalfields Lens and Douai. Therefore, Thomas served on the Western Front in the final phase of the War, when the tide was turned against Germany.

Thomas was demobilised from the Royal Garrison Artillery in January 1919. For his military service, he was awarded a campaign medal, the British War and Victory Medal. A second child, Thomas was born to him and Eva in 1920.

Of his military service, Thomas in later years would only ever say, 'nothing happened' and he was reluctant to elaborate further. The historical evidence suggests that Thomas's experience at the front was uneventful in comparison to earlier phases of the war marked by heavy losses of life, great suffering and hasty troop withdrawals. Thomas's brigade was spared casualties and did not retreat whilst he served with it. For him, nothing untoward happened. Nonetheless, it is evident that enemy firepower was directed at his brigade. Its personnel were confronted by the sights and sounds of regular shelling from the long range enemy guns that put them in danger. When Thomas recalled his time on the Western Front he always omitted the danger to which he was exposed and what he felt about it.

On his demobilisation, Thomas returned to his former job on the Advertiser. In 1926, most employees of D.C. Thomson were members of the trade union, NATSOPA and they participated in the general strike. Thomson was outraged at the effect the strike had on his business, and only allowed the NATSOPA members to return to work after they tendered a personal apology and signed an undertaking to say they had left the union and would not join any other. Many employees at D.C. Thomson, restarted on the terms that were offered and Thomas was one. The alternatives to working for D.C. Thomson in 1926 and afterwards were very unpromising because of the poor state of the economy. In return for severing their trade union membership, employees were comparatively well paid and given good conditions. In the aftermath of the general strike, D.C. Thomson amalgamated the Dundee Advertiser with the other local newspaper, the Courier, which became the name of the new amalgamated newspaper for which Thomas worked. In 1927, a third child, Sydney was born to Thomas and Eva.

Although Thomas was at odds with his employer in 1926, in subsequent years he became reconciled for he remained an employee until retirement. Security of employment with good pay removed the differences that he once had with D.C. Thomson. His promotion to foreman in later years may also have helped to change his opinion of his employer. In reality, Thomas and his employer shared a common outlook of strict Presbyterianism combined with conservativism. The dissenting United Free Church, in which he was married, eventually reunited with the Church of Scotland and he was for many years an elder of the Kirk. His Presbyterianism was sectarian in character, shown on a number of occasions when he expressed disapproval of members of his family being friends with either Episcopalians or Catholics. The sectarian Presbyterian viewpoint supported by Thomas and D.C. Thomson was graphically expressed in a report submitted to the General Assembly of the Church of Scotland in 1923 and known as 'The Menace of the Irish Race to our Scottish Nationality'.

D.C. Thomson was renowned for its conservatism, for it was largely based on paternalism, frugality, tight family control (often described as secretive) and staff loyalty. It was widely considered old-fashioned in many ways. It was as late as 1992, that the Dundee Courier became the last daily paper in Britain to put news, rather than adverts or notices on its front page. Its conservatism embraced not only hostility to trade unions but anti-Catholicism. D. C. Thomson steadfastly refused to employ Catholics, a position which was only quietly dropped in the 1950s.

Two particular occasions, demonstrated Thomas's Presbyterian conservative outlook. Thomas's daughter, Doris married George in 1937 and their first child, Eva, was born in 1938. When Thomas and Eva's became aware of the pre-marital conception of their first grandchild they ostracised their daughter and son-in-law for about a year. Thomas strongly disapproved of an affront to values that he considered inviolable. In 1950, Thomas's son, Thomas, married Flora Reid, who was an unmarried mother and Thomas and Eva eschewed contact with their new daughter- in- law. Eva opined that Flora was 'not one of us' and she and Thomas considered Flora's family disreputable, exemplified by them sheltering a son who had deserted from the army. The values of acceptable behaviour that Thomas held dear had been challenged by his son's marriage, so he and Eva showed their disapproval.

Notwithstanding his Presbyterianism and conservatism, Thomas possessed a humane outlook and a sense of humour. He supported the principle that all people were of equal value and deserved the same consideration when he frequently uttered the proverb, 'We're a' Jock Tamson's Bairns'. However, on occasion he felt he must give precedence to other precepts before equal consideration.

Thomas's conservative attitudes extended to politics. Although, in his early years, he voted Liberal, he was a Conservative voter for most of his life. He defended his support for the Conservative party on the grounds that its representatives were uniquely qualified to govern as a result of their education and standing in society. His deferential political viewpoint was characteristic of a working class Conservative.

In 1952, employees who had secretly become trade unionists were dismissed from D.C. Thomson. In 1953, the TUC organised a boycott of newspapers and comics published by D.C. Thomson because of its anti-union attitude. In support of the boycott, Thomas's son-in-law, George, substituted alternative comics for his children instead of the Thomson published *Beano* and *Dandy*.

Nevertheless, Thomas continued to post the *Sunday Post* and *People's Journal* to the Smith household in Manchester. There were long-standing political differences between Thomas and George but they avoided open conflict.

Thomas worked for thirty years on the night shift as an overseer in the pressroom of the Courier in the centre of Dundee. Because there was no public transport in the early hours of the morning when he finished work, he walked the two miles home and on the way, bought morning rolls for the household. In total, he had fifty three and a half years' service with the same employer, when he died in 1962.

Chapter 12

Gruelly Belkies

The inhabitants of the island of Sanday in Orkney were called gruelly belkies. In Orcadian dialect it meant porridge bellies or fat people. The nickname originated from a time when Sanday's agrarian fertility earned it the reputation as the granary of Orkney. The inhabitants of the other islands looked enviously at the gruelly belkies. The maternal ancestors of Thomas Sinclair Maxwell Drever were gruelly belkies for they lived on the island of Sanday in Orkney.

The island home of the gruelly belkies, Sanday, is the largest of the north isles of Orkney, lying north of Stronsay and south of North Ronaldsay. It is a fairly narrow and irregular island extending some 15 miles from south west to north east, with a peninsula stretching north from its centre. It has been likened to a lobster in shape. It is very low lying and acquired its name from the broad sandy beaches that fringe many of its long bays. It shares the Norse heritage of the other Orkney Islands as a farming community with a largely peasant population. Chapter 11 outlined that heritage. Given the low marriage rate between the people of the different Orkney islands for centuries and the remoteness of the islands, it seems most probable that the maternal forebears of Thomas Drever inhabited Sanday from its settlement by the Norse. They were cut from the same cloth as most Orkney islanders. Thomas's maternal forebears from 1700 numbered six in direct order of descent. They were, Elspeth Swann, Jean Linklater, Sibella Harvey, Janet Milne, Jane Towrie, and Ann Scott Peace.

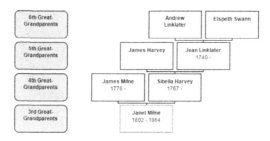

Elspeth Swan, Jean Linklater, Sibella Harvey

Only a few bare facts are known about Thomas Drever's early recorded maternal forebears. The earliest was Elspeth Swan. Elspeth Swann lived in the early 1700s. Elspeth's surname has several variants and they have firm Norse origins. The surname also has a long association with Sanday. Elspeth married Andrew Linklater and they had six children between 1740 and 1757. One incident occurred in Elspeth's life which is illuminative of the lives of ordinary Orcadians and Scots in general, at this time. In 1739, before their marriage, Elspeth and Andrew were accused of pre-marital sex and summoned to appear before the next meeting of the kirk session (church court). Whilst a record of the next meeting has not survived, the course of events that followed can be assumed from customary practice at the kirk session. Wrong-doers found guilty, were rebuked in front of the whole congregation and expected to profess grief and sorrow for their sin. Repentance, together with the payment of a fine of a few Scottish pounds, if exacted, absolved them from church censure.

It was the role of the Church of Scotland to exercise moral discipline in the local community, which concentrated to a great extent, on sexual misbehaviour. In the early 1700s, Calvinist dogma with its belief in man's innate sinfulness was the order of the day. The elders of the Church peered literally into the everyday activities of parishioners in their homes, workshops and barns to ensure that the moral order was upheld by all. Failure to appear before the church court could instigate action by justices of the peace. The Church had considerable powers that it could exercise over the lives of parishioners to secure compliance with its proscriptions. It was only in the late 1700s that the Churche's grip on social behaviour really loosened.

Jean Linklater was born in 1740. She married James Harvey and they had three children between 1761 and 1767.

Sibella Harvey, born in 1767, married James Milne, and they had six children between 1796 and 1813.

Sanday in the 1700s

As inhabitants of Sanday in the 1700s, these three female forebears belonged to a population of about eighteen hundred people who lived in three hundred and forty nine houses. The inhabitants of Sanday were outnumbered by the sheep that totalled over four thousand. Sanday's population, as in times past, was wholly engaged in agriculture, there being only a few employed in other trades such as weaving and shoemaking. In the 1790s, there were forty seven tenant farmers. The rest of the population were peasants, if young, attached to farms as servants and if older, labourers with smallholdings of land that varied in size. The landowners were few in number, absentees, largely uninterested in their estates.

The crops grown were principally barley, oats, potatoes, cabbage and turnips. Swine and cattle were also reared. The farm horses on Sanday totalled five hundred and thirty three, a greater number than for any other island in Orkney and a very large proportion of the total farm horse population of all the islands of Orkney. The large farm horse population of Sanday indicates an important economic activity – seaweed collection. Horses were used to collect the seaweed both to fertilise the soil and to make kelp. The seaweed was collected in wooden creels placed on either side of the horses and the bottoms could be opened to distribute the seaweed onto the ground. Sanday was perhaps the most fertile of all the Orkney Islands and that fertility owed much to the seaweed that greatly helped in the cultivation of the crops. Kelp was also made from the seaweed and sold for use outside the island in several industrial processes such as glass making. Of all the kelp made in the Orkney isles, Sanday produced almost a quarter. Although Sanday derived great economic benefits from seaweed, it was not immune from adverse economic circumstances during the 1700s. For example, in 1782-83 poor harvests caused great hardship but not the loss of life from famine that had occurred during the 1600s.

A glimpse of the lives of Elspeth Swan, Jean Linklater and Sibella Harvey is suggested by the historical evidence about the inhabitants of Sanday in the 1700s. Young women were often farm servants with domestic chores as their principal responsibilities. These responsibilities could include the care of the farmer's young children, cooking for the household and spinning yarn for it also. The outdoor work of female farm servants was working in the fields, doing much the same work as men. Women were paid less than men and payment was often largely in kind. For domestic servants, payment could be by small articles, such as shoes as well as cash.

In the households of the agricultural population, women, were heavily involved in the making of kelp, through burning the seaweed, not a pleasant task. This activity was undertaken during the summer months, in between spring and harvest time. In winter, they were busy in making clothes for the family. The clothes were coarse and made from wool and from linen. The wool came from the handful of sheep that a peasant household reared. The linen was spun and woven from the flax that was imported into Sanday. Women also engaged in the various tasks associated with the plot of land which was held by a peasant household. When there was a cow, it was the women who looked after it, milked it and turned the milk into butter. It was women who were responsible for making two sources of fuel for the home. They gathered the sea weed and dried it and made the cow dung into balls which was dried and then ready for use in the domestic hearth. There was no coal and peat could only be obtained by paying to dig it up on a nearby island and transporting it by boat home. Women participated in cultivating the plot of land and harvesting the cabbages, onions, carrots, and parsnips that had been sown. Women also participated in the hunting expeditions to capture and slaughter whales when shoals came close inshore. The whales provided valuable resources for domestic use.

A further source of fuel for the home came from shipwrecks on Sanday. Many ships foundered on the island's reefs and rocks, unable to see the shore. Five thousand tons of shipping was wrecked on the island between 1773 and 1790. Only when a lighthouse was completed in 1807 did the problem lessen. The shipwrecks provided the Sanday population with wood, there being no local supply for Sanday in common with the rest of the Orkney islands, was treeless.

The homes that were inhabited by the mass of the Sanday people in the 1700s were typically long houses with animals accommodated in one end and people in the other end. The roof was made of heather and straw and there was a smoke hole. These houses were not warm or comfortable and the climate was moist and raw. People typically lived in close knit communities called townships that were clusters of dwellings surrounded by a complex strip patchwork of arable land that was peculiar to Orkney and Sheltand.

In the 1700s Orcadians were ceasing to speak Norn or Old Norse and English became universal with many words in use of Scandinavian origin. For Elspeth, Jean and Sibella, three schools existed on Sanday in the 1700s but there were only eight free school places. Generally in Scotland, females had restricted access to schooling and their literacy was much lower than that of males. In schools, cultural values dictated that girls' learning be limited to practical skills.

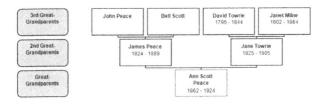

Janet Milne

Janet Milne was born in 1802 and died in 1864. She married David Towrie, and they had seven girls between 1825 and 1842. David Towrie was both a smallholder and a joiner. It was not unusual for some peasants to combine their agricultural activities with a trade. In its later years, the household of Janet Milne and David Towrie had two and a half acres of land. The small size of the plot suggests that it was insufficient to provide subsistence for the needs of the family on its own. Therefore, joinery and farm labouring tasks were undertaken for farmers and others on Sanday to sustain a sufficient standard of living.

In 1844, Janet was widowed when David Towrie, aged forty eight, died. Janet took over the plot and her elder sister, Jane, joined the household to help out. Jane had been living in the household of her married brother Thomas. If Janet could have afforded the fees, her daughters may have attended the sole parochial school on Sanday. Its pupils numbered fifty three, from the island population of eighteen hundred. Janet's daughters' time was most likely to have been spent on helping in the household and on the family's plot of land. By 1861, all the daughters had left home and had apparently entered domestic service. In her later years, Janet lived with her daughter Jemima, her fisherman son-in- law and their three children.

Jane Towrie

Jane Towrie was born in 1825, married James Peace and they had six children between 1850 and 1867. Jane's husband, James Peace, was a small holder and a mason. As a mason, he was one of five in the trade on the island. By 1861, his small holding at Stratigarth, amounted to six acres, Jane helped to run their small holding that grew into a small farm. Domestic and agricultural tasks fully occupied her throughout her life. Jane's younger sister Jemima was also a member of the household for a time and worked on the farm. The second child of Jane and James, born in 1852, was baptised into the Free Church of Scotland which suggests that they transferred their loyalty from the Church of Scotland, albeit only provisionally.

As the children grew older, they were able to provide labour for Jane and James's farm. Even so, it was also necessary for a labourer to be hired, particularly by 1881 when the farm had grown in size to seventeen acres. After the death of her husband James in 1889, Jane remained on the family farm, the tenancy of which had passed to her son John and he and his wife were now in charge of it. John had followed his father in combining the trade of a mason with that of farming. Jane's daughter, Janet, also remained on the farm. By 1901, the family farm utilised the labour of Jane's daughter Christina and husband James, an agricultural labourer. After Jane's death in 1905, her son John, continued as the tenant of the farm, helped by his wife.

The six sisters of Jane Towrie, like her, had lives in domestic and farm service on Sanday. Later in their lives, two of the sisters departed from this norm, however. Sibella migrated to Leith in her fifties, some years after being widowed. She joined one of her sons there, who was a shipwright. Margaret, married a farmer of a few acres, who also had the trade of shoemaker. About 1893, Margaret, her husband James Scott and their adult children migrated to Dundee. For Margaret and James, Dundee became the place for their retirement. For the six children that accompanied them, (one being Jane, a single parent of a daughter, Olivia born in 1891) it offered good prospects for employment in contrast to rural Sanday.

Sanday in the 1800s

Kelp-making declined in the Orkney Isles because of the introduction of substitutes and by 1830 the industry was in a state of collapse. The reliance on kelp-making meant that there was an adverse impact on the whole community with some small landowners made bankrupt. To substitute for the loss of income, fishing became an important commercial activity that was taken up by small tenants and cottars. Cod, herring, skate, ling and lobster were harvested from the sea for export. Kelp making did not cease entirely, however. As in the 1700s, Sanday's economy still relied on the production of crops, barley and oats particularly, for export. Cattle, sheep in large numbers as well as pigs continued to be reared. Farm servants were only employed for two thirds of the year for they were engaged in fishing for the rest of it. Many female farm servants were engaged in the plaiting of straw for bonnets. Much land, formerly considered as unsuitable for cultivation was reclaimed.

Ann Scott Peace

Ann Scott Peace was born in 1862, one of six siblings, of whom one died in infancy. Ann and her younger sister, Christina, were of school age when elementary education for all children in Scotland between the ages of five and thirteen was made compulsory in 1872. Schooling was provided for pupils on Sanday and the island of North Ronaldsay by four teachers. After leaving school, Ann followed a customary path for girls on Sanday by becoming a domestic servant. She married Charles Drever in 1884.

Ann was the only one of her siblings to leave Orkney. The others lived their whole lives on Sanday. Ann's sister Janet, a dressmaker and single woman, departed from convention on the island when she became an unmarried mother to three children, one of whom died in infancy. Unmarried mothers were stigmatised but by continuing to live on the family farm, Janet could count on the support of her parents and siblings in contending with ostracism. In 1897, several years after the births of her children, Janet married a blacksmith and small farmer, twenty one years her senior. He had been a widower for a year and had no children from his previous marriage. Ann's sister Isabella, a domestic servant, married John Drever, agricultural labourer and the brother of Charels Drever, Ann's husband. Ann's brother John, remained the tenant of the small family farm at Stratigarth during his life. Ann's sister, Christina, a domestic servant married a farm servant in 1894 and he died in 1902. She re-married another farm servant in 1912. On Sanday, Ann's siblings lived near to each other for most of their lives.

Ann left Sanday in 1898 when she and her husband, Charles Drever, migrated to Dundee. For Ann and Charles, the choice of Dundee and the process of settling in may have been facilitated by family ties. For Ann's aunt and uncle, Margaret Towrie and James Scott had been settled there since 1893. In 1901 in Dundee, these relatives lived less than a mile, or a walk of fifteen minutes, from the address of Ann and Charles. Therefore Ann and Charles may have been helped to adjust from rural Sanday to urban Dundee by their relatives.

Ann's life after her marriage in 1884 is described in chapter 11.

Bibliography

This bibliography includes the principal sources consulted for this book but omits those of lesser importance. Besides the publications listed below, the Web has provided many sources of invaluable information. Of these sources, Ancestry UK, Electric Scotland, Friends of Dundee City Archives, Orkney Family History Society, Scotlands People and Tay Valley Family History Society have been particularly helpful.

Allan, V. L. *Power in Trade Unions*, London, 1954.

Andrew, C. *The Defence of the Realm: The Authorized History of MI5*, London, 2009.

Angus Archives, MS 61/1/2 National Union of Boot and Shoe Operatives, Arbroath Branch minutes, 1900-1908.

Angus Archives, MS 61/1/3 National Union of Boot and Shoe Operatives, Arbroath Branch minutes 1909-1918.

Angus Archives, MS 88/1/2 Arbroath Independent Labour Party, minute book 1920-1925.

Arbroath Guide.

Arbroath Herald.

Arbroath Yearbook.

Bamfield, V. *On the Strength*, London, 1974.

Bathurst, B. *The Lighthouse Stevensons*, London, 2005.

Baxter, P. *Perth Its weavers and weaving*, Perth, 1936.

Beckett, F. *Enemy Within*, London, 1995.

Beckett, I.F.W. *Britain's Part-Time Soldiers*, Barnsley, 2011.

Bigwood, R. *The Scottish Family Tree Detective*, Manchester, 2006.

Black, G.F. *The Surnames of Scotland, Their Origin, Meaning and History,* New York, 1946.

Bremner, D. *The industries of Scotland; their rise, progress and present condition*, Edinburgh, 1869.

Brims, J. D. *The Scottish Democratic Movement in the Age of the French Revolution*, PhD thesis, University of Edinburgh,1983.

British Association, Dundee, 1912 Handbook and Guide to Dundee and District, Dundee, 1912.

Brown, W. *Early Days in a Dundee Mill 1819-1823,* Dundee, 1980.

Burman, B. *Seamstresses.*

Castle, B. *The Castle Diaries 1964-1970*, London, 1984.

Castle, B. *The Castle Diaries 1974-1976*, London, 1980.

Clegg, H. A. *A History of British Trade Unions since 1889* Vol 111 1934-1951, Oxford, 1994.

Colley, L. *Britons, Forging the Nation 1707-1837*, New Haven and London, 1992.

Connelly, T.J. *The Woodworkers 1860-1960*, London, 1960.

D'Arcy, H. *A bible of discontent*, 2013.

Davey, N. & Perkins, J. *Broughty Ferry Village to Suburb*, Dundee, 1976.

De Groot, G. *Back in Blighty, The British at home in World War One*, London, 2014.

Devine, T. M. *Clearance and Improvement Land, Power and People in Scotland 1700-1900*, Edinburgh, 2006.

Devine, T. M. *Farm Servants and Labour in Lowland Scotland 1770-1914*, Edinburgh, 1984.

Devine, T. *The Scottish Nation 1700 – 2007*, London, 2006.

Dowse, R.E. *Left in the Centre, The Independent Labour Party 1893-1940*, London, 1966.

Druker, J. *'One Big Union' Structural Change in Building Trade Unionism*, PhD thesis, University of Warwick, 1980.

Dundee Central Library, NRA(S) 1675 Dundee Harbour Porters minutes 1844-1887.

Dundee City Archive and Record Centre, GB251/GD/DH, Dundee Harbour Trust, 1814-1982.

Dundee City Archives, MS 158 Dundee Harbour Porters Philanthropic Society Petition 1873.

Dundee Directories.

Durie, B. *Scottish Genealogy*, Stroud, 2012.

Emm, A. *Tracing your Trade & Craftsman Ancestors*, Barnsley, 2015.

Fenton, A. *The Northern Isles: Orkney and Shetland*, Edinburgh, 1978.

Fox, A. *A History of the National Union of Boot and Shoe Operatives 1874-1957*, Oxford, 1958.

Foyster, E. & Whatley, C. eds. *A History of Everyday Life in Scotland: 1660 to 1800*, Edinburgh, 2010.

Fraser, B. *The Scottish Jutewallah.*

Fraser, W. H. & Morris, R.J. *People and Society in Scotland 1830-1914*, Edinburgh, 1990.

Friends of Dundee City Archives, The Staple Trade of Dundee.

Griffiths. T. & Morton, G. *A History of Everyday Life in Scotland 1800 to 1900*, Edinburgh, 2010.

Groome, F.H. ed. *Ordnance Gazetteer of Scotland: A Survey of Scottish Topography, Statistical, Biographical and Historical*, Edinburgh, 1884-1885.

Hannay Thompson, J. and others, *Dundee Harbour Trust 1830-1930*, Dundee.

Hannay Thompson, J. & Richie G. *Dundee Harbour Trust Official Handbook 1933*, London.

Hobsbawm, E. J. *Labouring Men, Studies in the History of Labour*, London, 1964.

Honeyman, V. *'That ye may judge for yourselves': The contribution of Scottish Presbyterianism towards the emergence of political awareness amongst ordinary people in Scotland between 1746 and 1792*, PhD thesis, University of Stirling, 2012.

Houston, R. A. & Whyte, I.D. eds. *Scottish Society 1500-1800*, Cambridge, 1989.

Jackson, G. & Kinnear, K. *The Trade and Shipping of Dundee 1750-1850*, Dundee, 1991.

Jeffrey, A. *This Dangerous Menace*, Edinburgh, 1991.

Kingsford, P.W. *Victorian Railwaymen*, 1970, London.

Lenman, B. and others, *Dundee and its Textile Industry 1850-1914*, Dundee, 1969.

Light, A. *Common People*, London, 2014.

Lythe, S.G.E. Early Days of the Arbroath and Forfar Railway, *Railway Magazine*, January 1953.

Mackie, C. Historical Description of the town of Dundee, Glasgow, 1836._

Malcolm, J. *The Parish of Monfieth in Ancient and Modern Times*, Edinburgh, 1910.

Marshall, T. H. *The History of Perth from the Earliest Period to the Present Time*, Perth, 1849.

Marshall, W. Historic Scenes in Forfarshire, Edinburgh, 1875.

Martin, R. M. *TUC: The Growth of a Pressure Group 1868-1976*, Oxford, 1980.

McDermott, J. *British Military Service Tribunals 1916-1918*, Manchester, 2011.

Meikle, H. W. *Scotland and the French Revolution*, Glasgow, 1912.

Milligan, S. *The New Barons*, London, 1976.

Mtichison, R. *The Old Poor Law in Scotland*, Edinburgh, 2000.

Modern Records Centre, University of Warwick, Amalgamated Society of Woodworkers Collection.

Modern Records Centre, University of Warwick, Trades Union Congress Collection.

Modern Records Centre, University of Warwick, Union of Construction Allied Trades and Technicians Collection.

Morrison, A. *The Defence of Scotland – Militias, Fencibles and Volunteer Corps 1793-1820.*

Murray, N. *A social history of the Scottish Handloom weavers 1790-1850*, PhD thesis, University of Strathclyde, 1976.

National Library of Scotland, *Broadside Regarding Highland Soldiers and their Mutiny in Glasgow* 1795.

National Library of Scotland, Ordnance Survey large scale town maps 1847-1895.

National Records of Scotland, CH2/505, Record of Arbirlot Kirk Session 1709-1998.

National Records of Scotland, GD 16/52/25, Monthly list and muster roll of the Fourth Regiment of Fencibles, First Battalion.

'New' Statistical Account of Scotland (1834-1845).

'Old' Statistical Account of Scotland (1791-1799).

Penny, G. *Traditions of Perth*, Perth, 1836.

Penny, J. The Severn District Sea Fencibles 1803-1810, *Regional Historian* Issue 6, Autumn/Winter 2002.

Perth and Kinross Council Archives, MS 14/16 Miscellaneous Deposits: Thomas Murie, Perthshire Milita.

Perth and Kinross Council Archives, PE66/Bundle 20, Certificates authorising the payment of allowances to the wives and children of men serving in the Perthshire Militia.

Perth Directories.

Perthshire Diary December 1st 1794 Breadalbane's Fencible Mutiny.

Platt, R. *Smuggling in the British Isles A history*, Stroud, 2007.

Prebble, J. *Mutiny, Highland Regiments in Revolt 1743-1804*, London, 1975.

Rendall, E. *Lest We Forget A History of Westray*, Kirkwall, 1987.

Royal Commission on Labour in 1893, *The Agricultural Labourer*, HMSO.

ScotlandsPlaces, Farm horse tax, 1797-8 Images of the original records for Arbirlot: •NRS ref. E326/10/3/64 •NRS ref. E326/10/9/158.

ScotlandsPlaces. Hearth tax records 1691-1695, Hearth tax records for Perthshire Vol 2, E69/19/2/64.

Small, R. *History of the Congregations of the United Presbyterian Church from 1733 to 1900*, Vol 2, Edinburgh, 1904.

Smout, T.C. *A Century of the Scottish People, 1830-1950*, London, 1986.

Smout, T.C. *A History of the Scottish People, 1560-1830*, London, 1969.

Stornoway Historical Society, A bit of a mystery Arnish Lighthouse.

Taylor, J. *The Great Historic Families of Scotland*: The Maules, 1887.

Taylor, R. *From the general strike to new unionism*, Basingstoke, 2000.

The Jutewallahs of Dundee.

The National Archives, WO/95/539/4 Army Troops, 11th Brigade, Royal Garrison Artillery, War Diary January to November 1918.

The National Archives ADM 175/3, Admiralty, predecessors and successors: Coastguard and predecessors: Records of Service, 1816-1947.

The National Archives, Records of the Coastguard ADM 175 Scotland 1822-1862 ADM 175/22.

The National Archives, ADM 28/104, Navy Board: Sea Fencibles Pay Lists, Coast of Angus, 1803-1804.

The National Archives, ADM 28/105, Navy Board: Sea Fencibles Pay Lists, Coast of Angus, 1806-1810.

The National Archives, ADM 29, Admiralty: Royal Navy, Royal Marines, Coastguard and related services: Officers' and Ratings' Service Records, 1802-1919.

The National Archives, WO 13/3810, Monthly pay lists and muster roll, Fourth Regiment of Breadalbane Fencibles Infantry, First Battalion.

The National Archives, WO 13/3912, Orkney and Shetland militia and volunteers pay lists and muster rolls 1793-1800.

The National Archives, WO 13/4488, Orkney and Shetland militia and volunteers muster books and pay lists 1804-1814.

Thompson, J. The History of Dundee, Dundee, 1874

Thomson, W. P. L. *Orkney Land and People*, Kirkwall 2008.

Tomlinson, J. & Whatley C. A. eds. *Jute No More*, Dundee, 2011.

Tomlinson, J. Dundee and the Empire: Juteopolis 1850-1939, Edinburgh, 2014.

Transactions of the Highland and Agricultural Society of Scotland On the Agriculture of the Counties of Forfar and Kincardine Fourth Series Vol X111 1881.

Tullibardine, Marchioness *A Military History of Perthshire 1660-1902*, Perth, 1908.

Turner, W.H.K. *Textile Industry of Arbroath since the early 18th Century*, Dundee, 1954.

Undy, R. and others, *Change in Trade Unions*, London, 1981.

Wallace, D.R. *The Romance of Jute A short history of the Calcutta Jute Mill Industry 1855-1927*, Calcutta, 1909.

Waller, I. H. *My Ancestor was an Agricultural Labourer*, London, 2010.

Waller, I. *My Ancestor was a Leather Worker*, London, 2015.

Waller, I. *My Ancestor was in the Royal Navy*, London, 2014.

Warden, A.J. - Angus or Forfarshire: the Land and People, Descriptive and Historical 5 vols, Dundee, 1880-85.

Warden, A.J. *The linen trade, ancient and modern*, London, 1867.

Webster, C. *What's in a name? A Street History of Broughty Ferry*, Dundee, 2014.

Wilcox, M. *Fishing and Fishermen A Guide for Family Historians*, Barnsley, 2009.

Wolmar, C. *Fire & Steam A New History of the Railways in Britain*, 2007, London.

Wood, L. W. *A Union to Build*, London, 1979.

Printed in Great Britain
by Amazon

24299645R00136